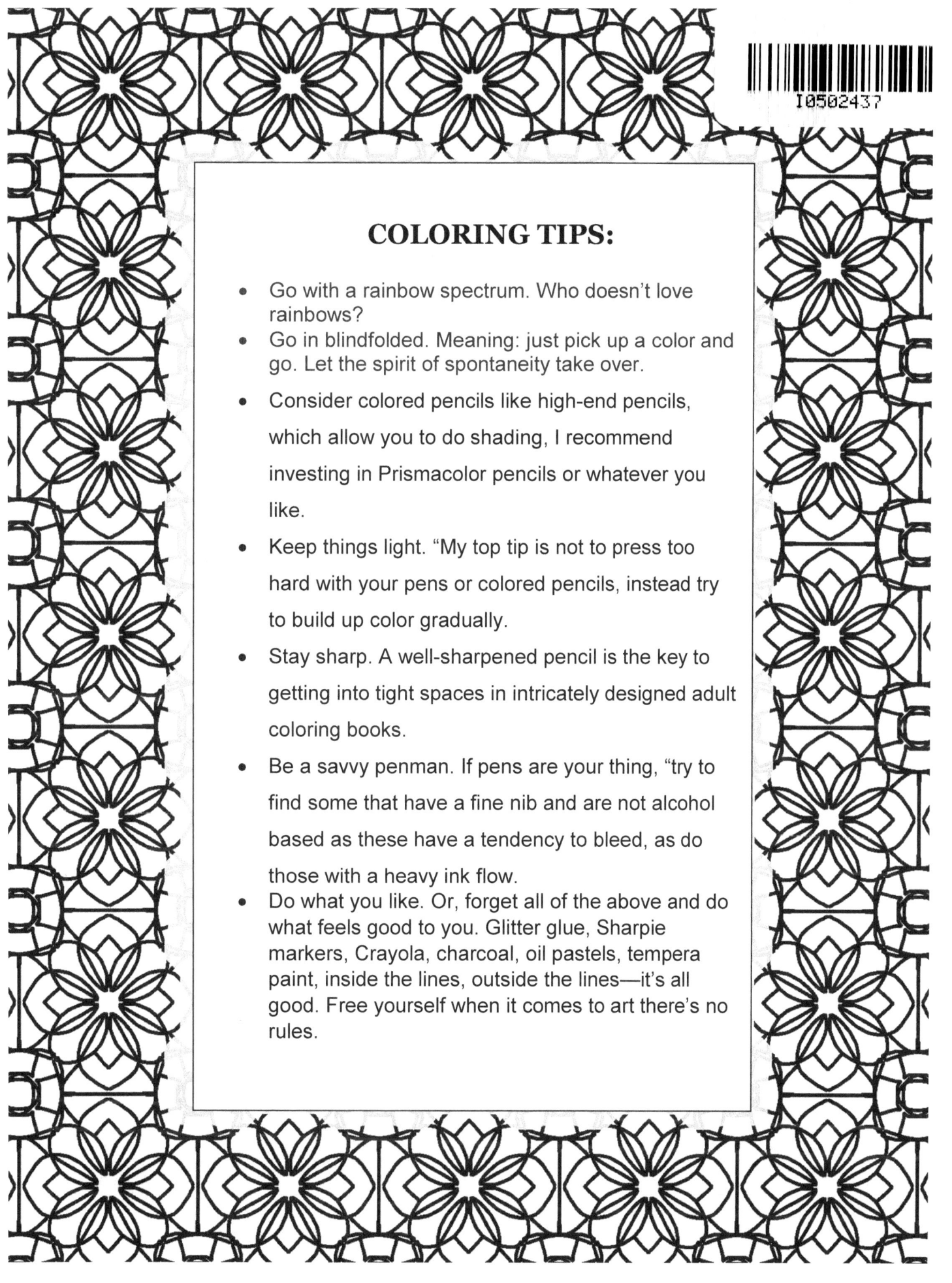

COLORING TIPS:

- Go with a rainbow spectrum. Who doesn't love rainbows?
- Go in blindfolded. Meaning: just pick up a color and go. Let the spirit of spontaneity take over.

- Consider colored pencils like high-end pencils, which allow you to do shading, I recommend investing in Prismacolor pencils or whatever you like.

- Keep things light. "My top tip is not to press too hard with your pens or colored pencils, instead try to build up color gradually.

- Stay sharp. A well-sharpened pencil is the key to getting into tight spaces in intricately designed adult coloring books.

- Be a savvy penman. If pens are your thing, "try to find some that have a fine nib and are not alcohol based as these have a tendency to bleed, as do those with a heavy ink flow.

- Do what you like. Or, forget all of the above and do what feels good to you. Glitter glue, Sharpie markers, Crayola, charcoal, oil pastels, tempera paint, inside the lines, outside the lines—it's all good. Free yourself when it comes to art there's no rules.

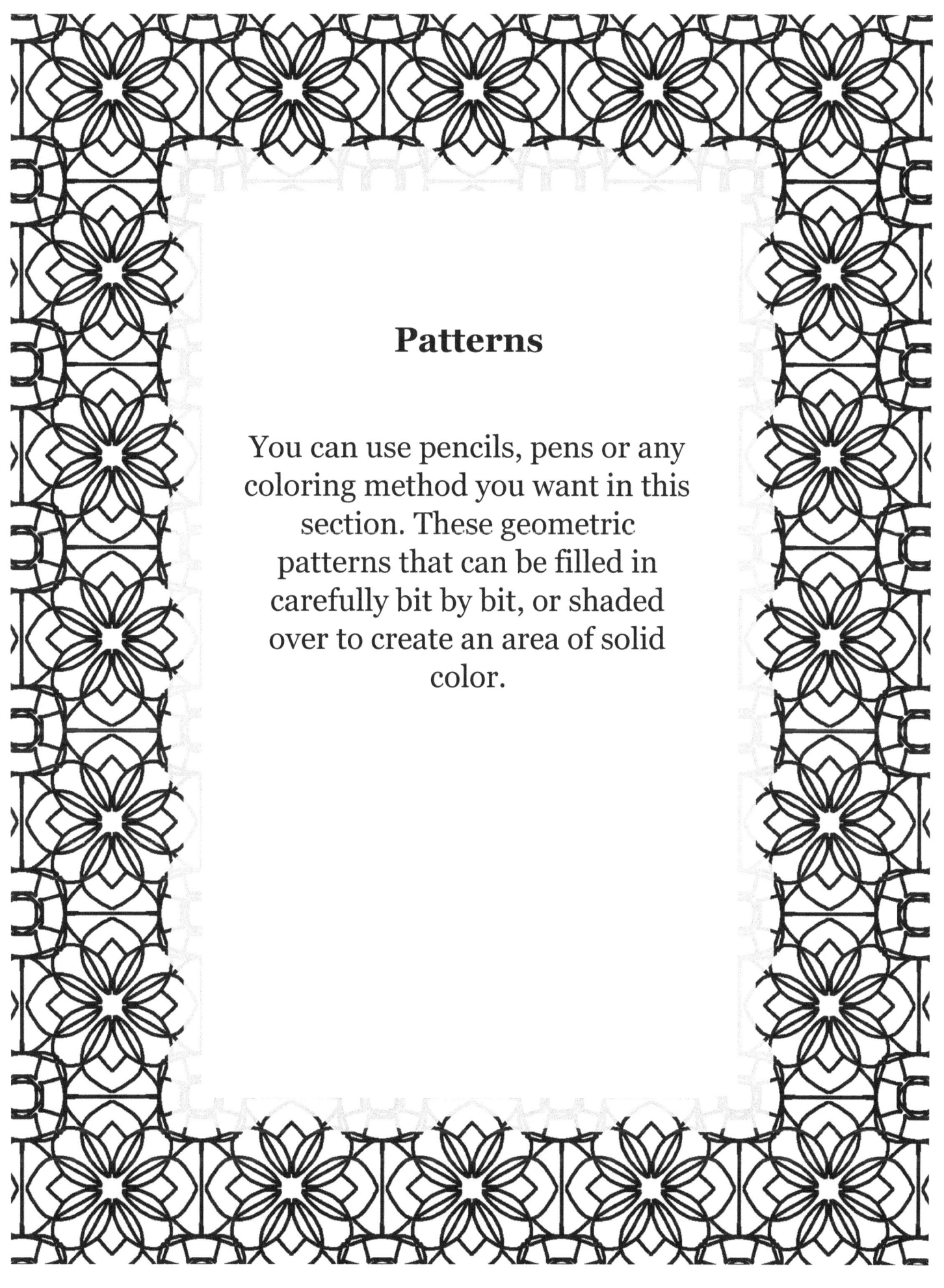

Patterns

You can use pencils, pens or any coloring method you want in this section. These geometric patterns that can be filled in carefully bit by bit, or shaded over to create an area of solid color.

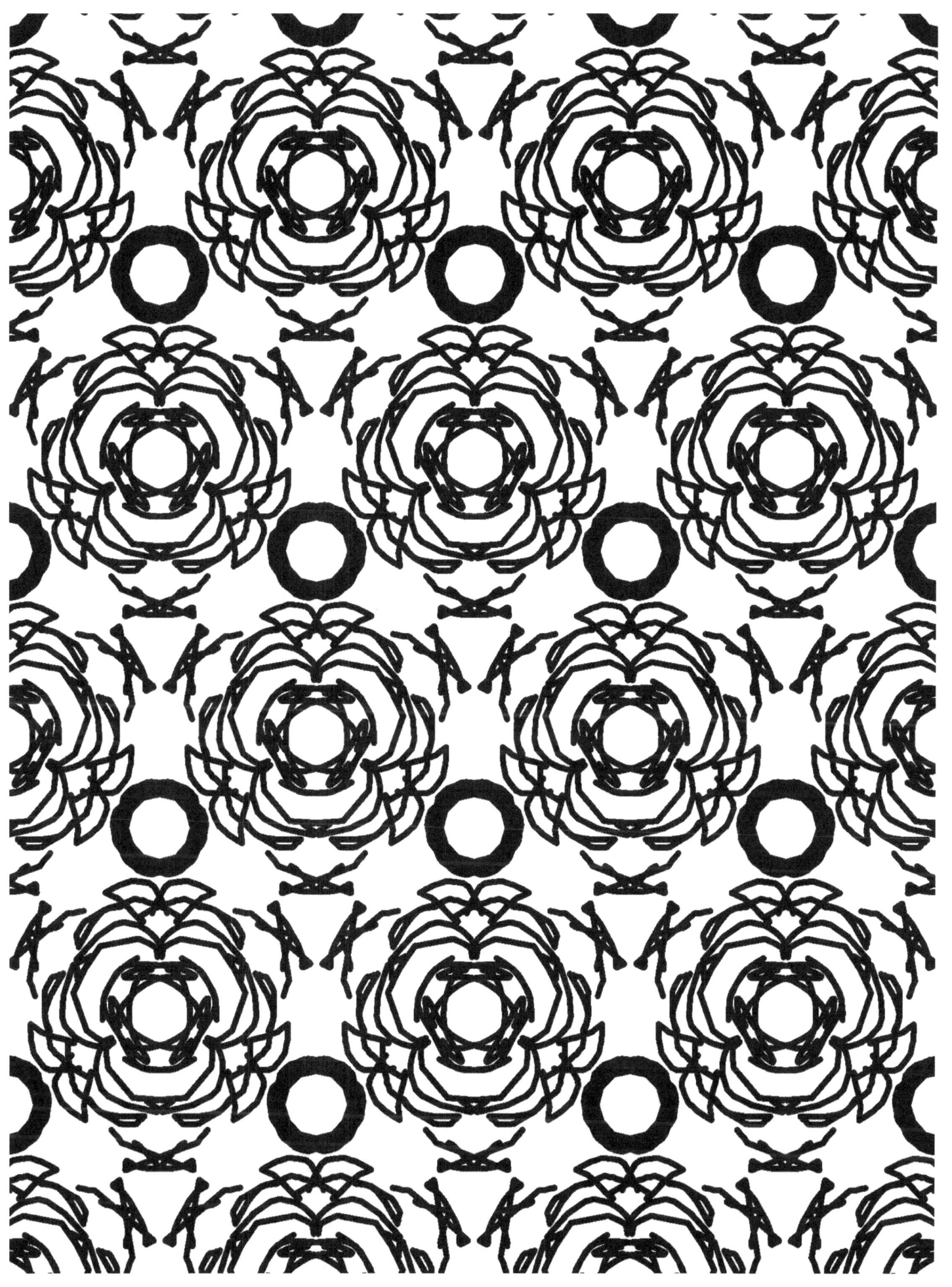

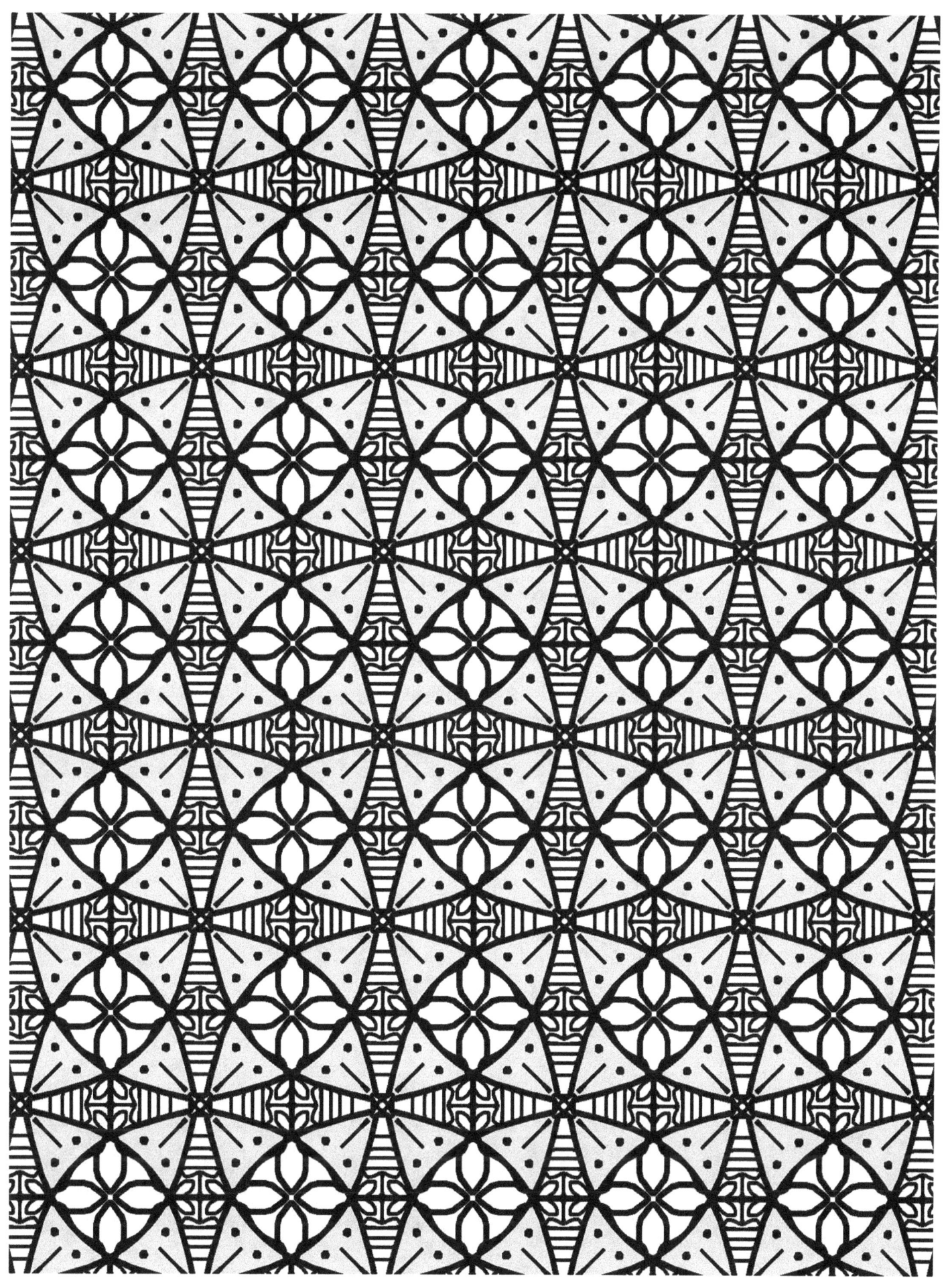

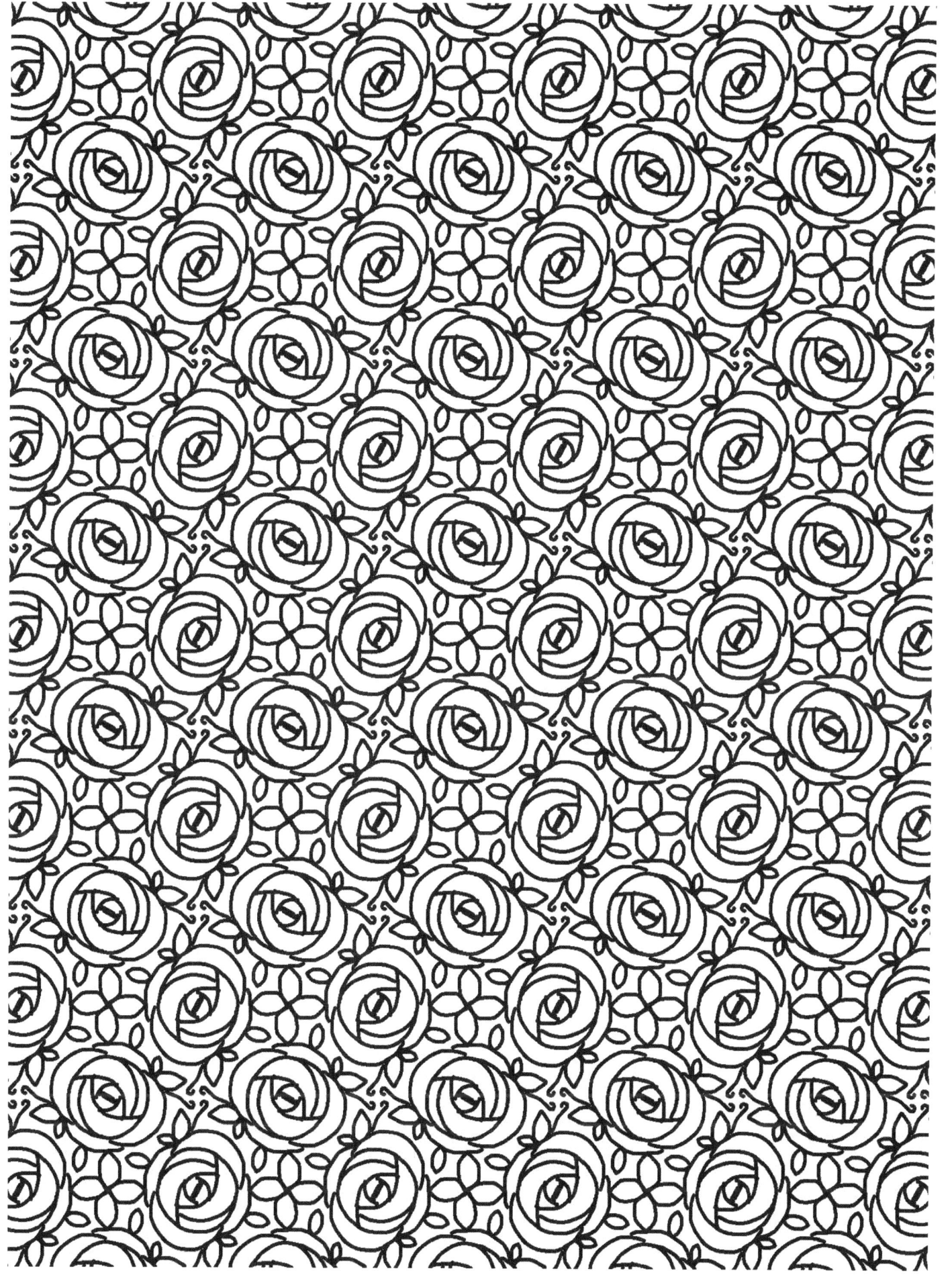

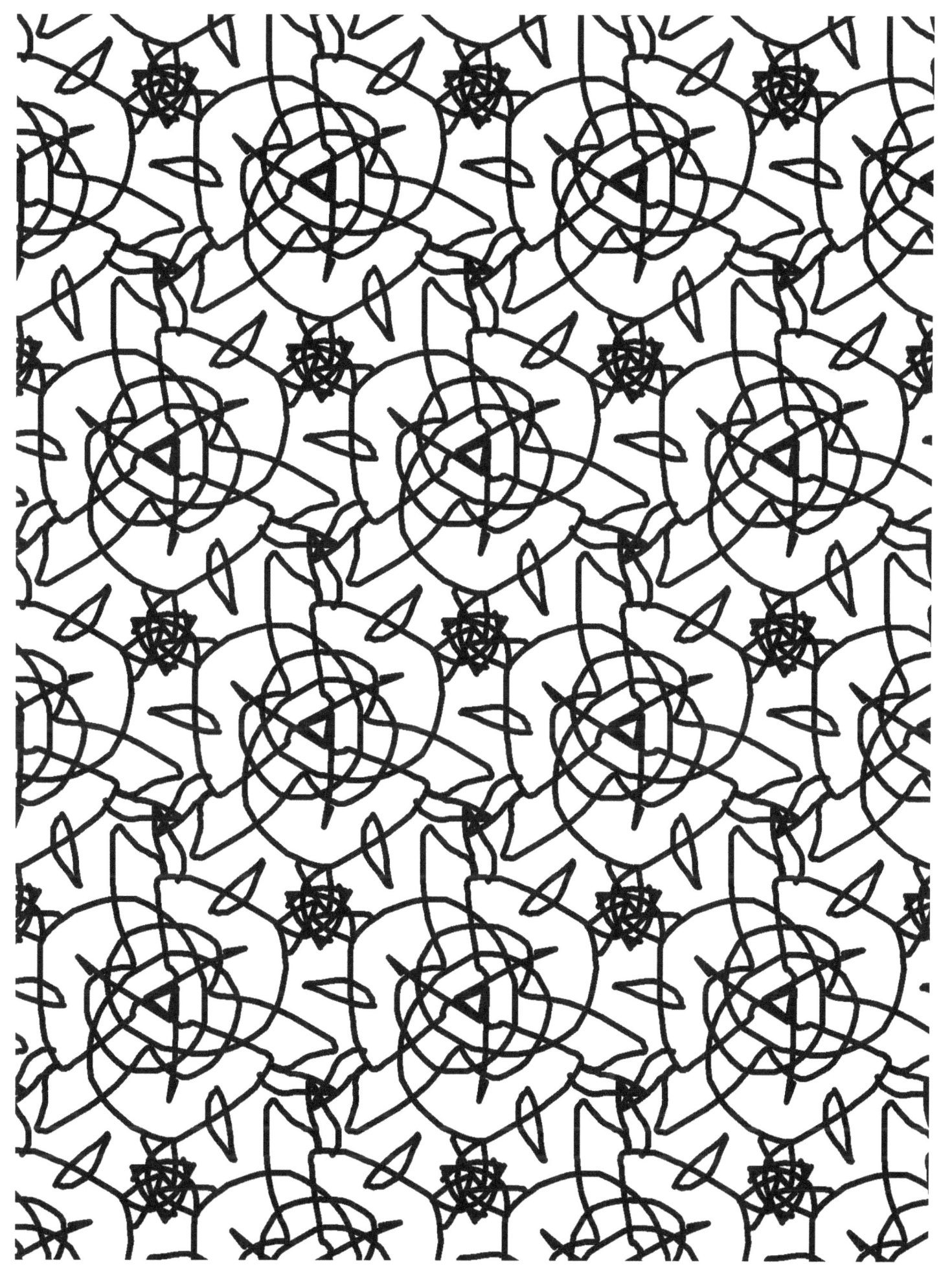

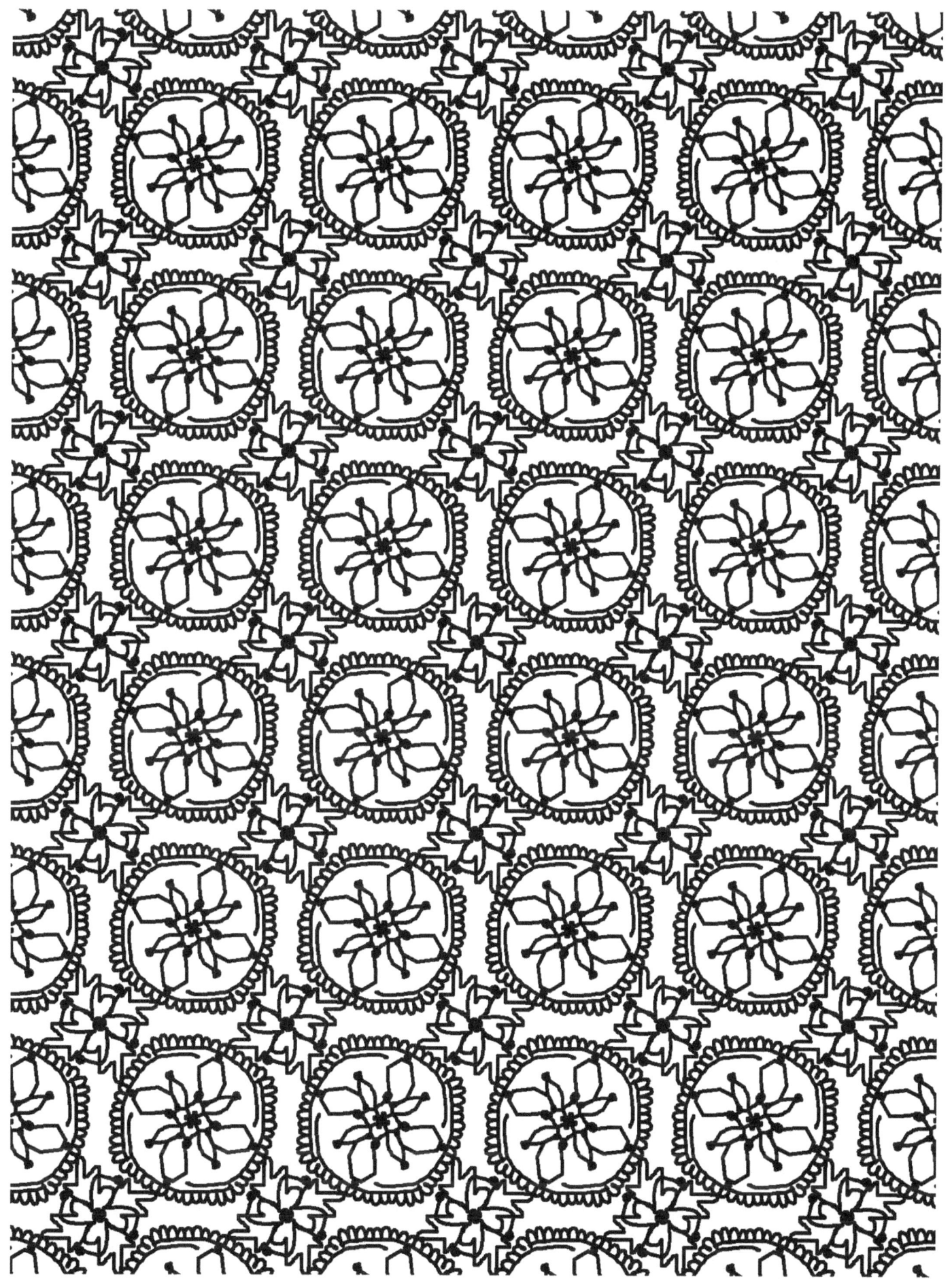

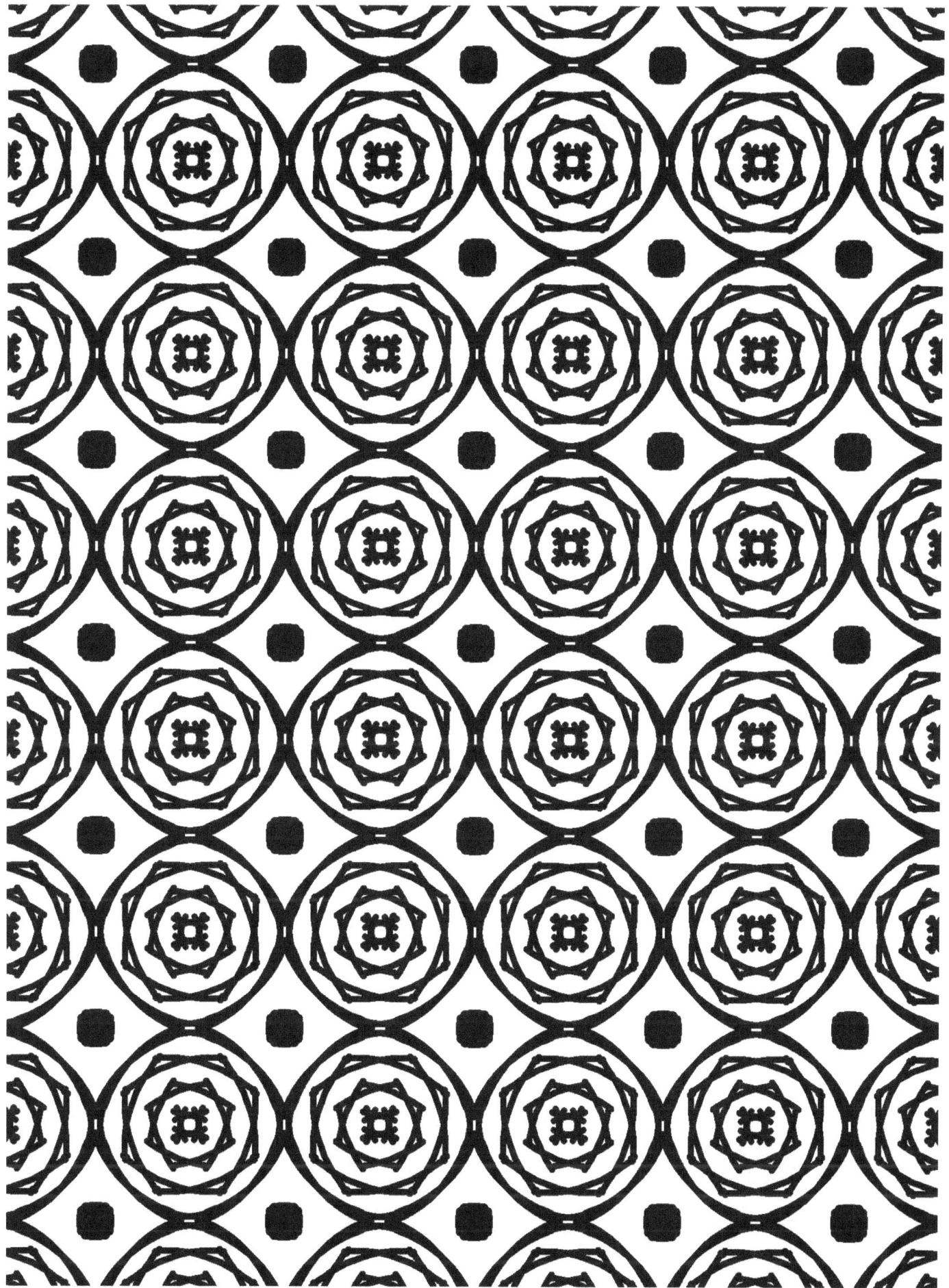

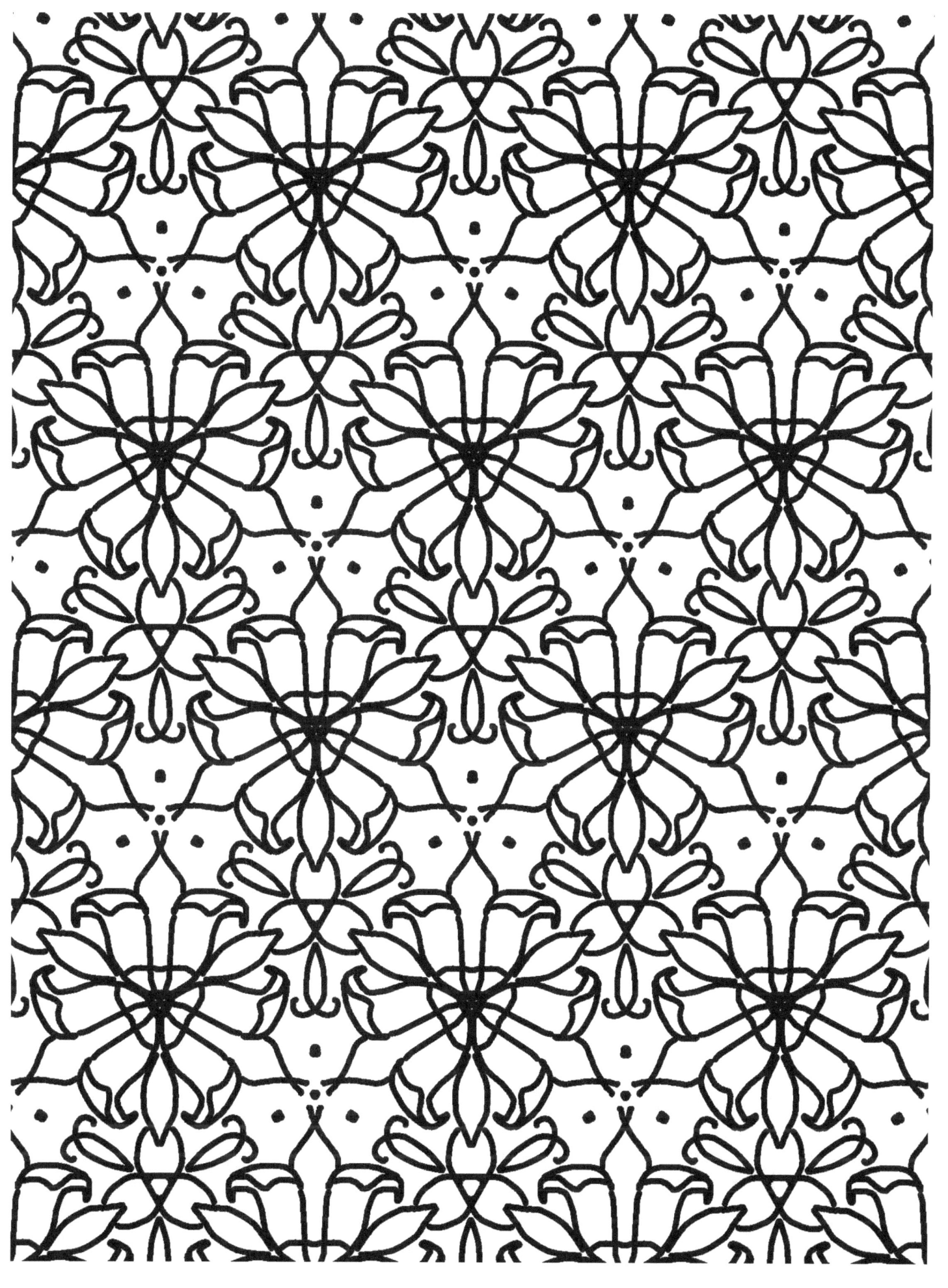

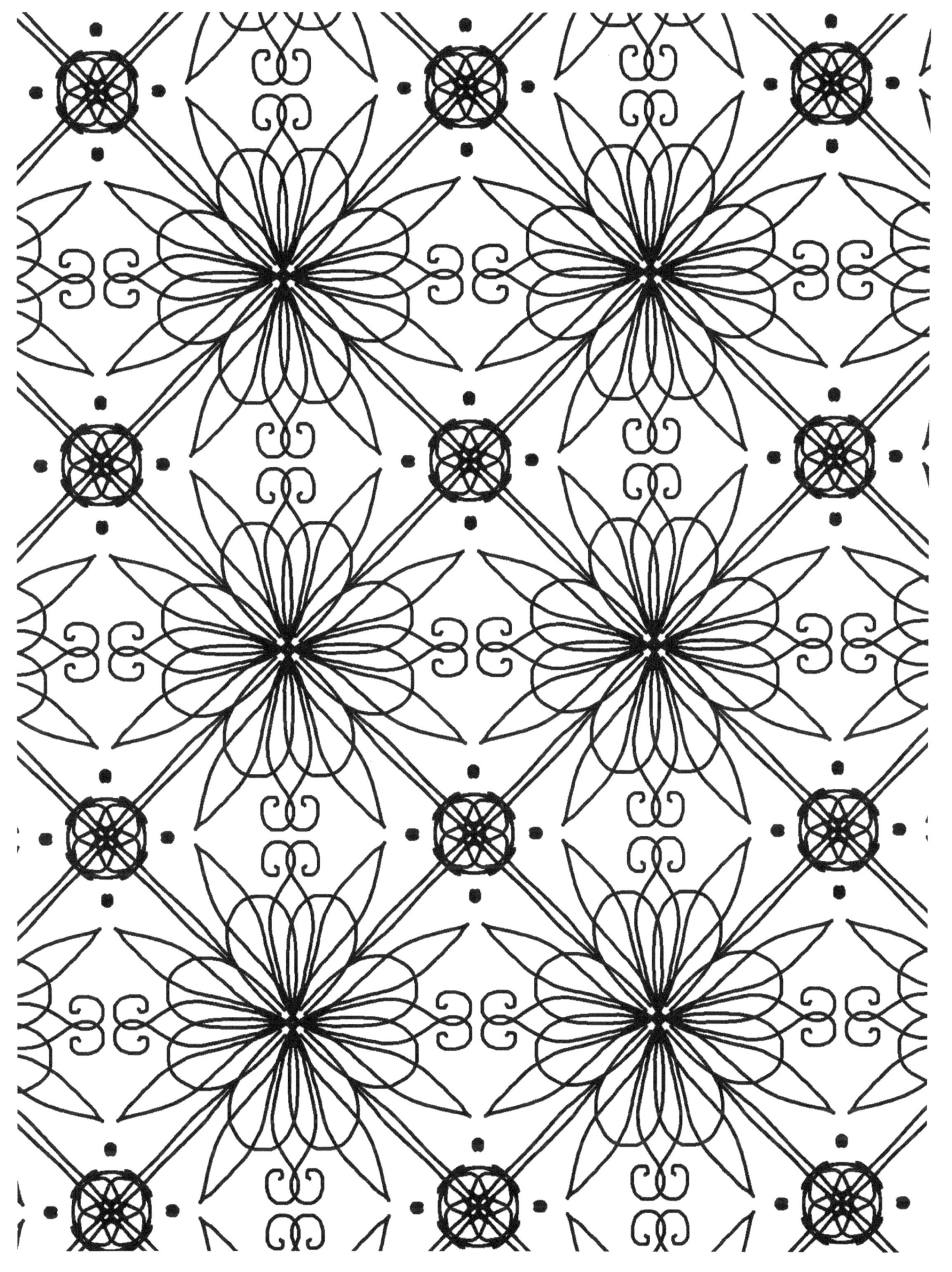

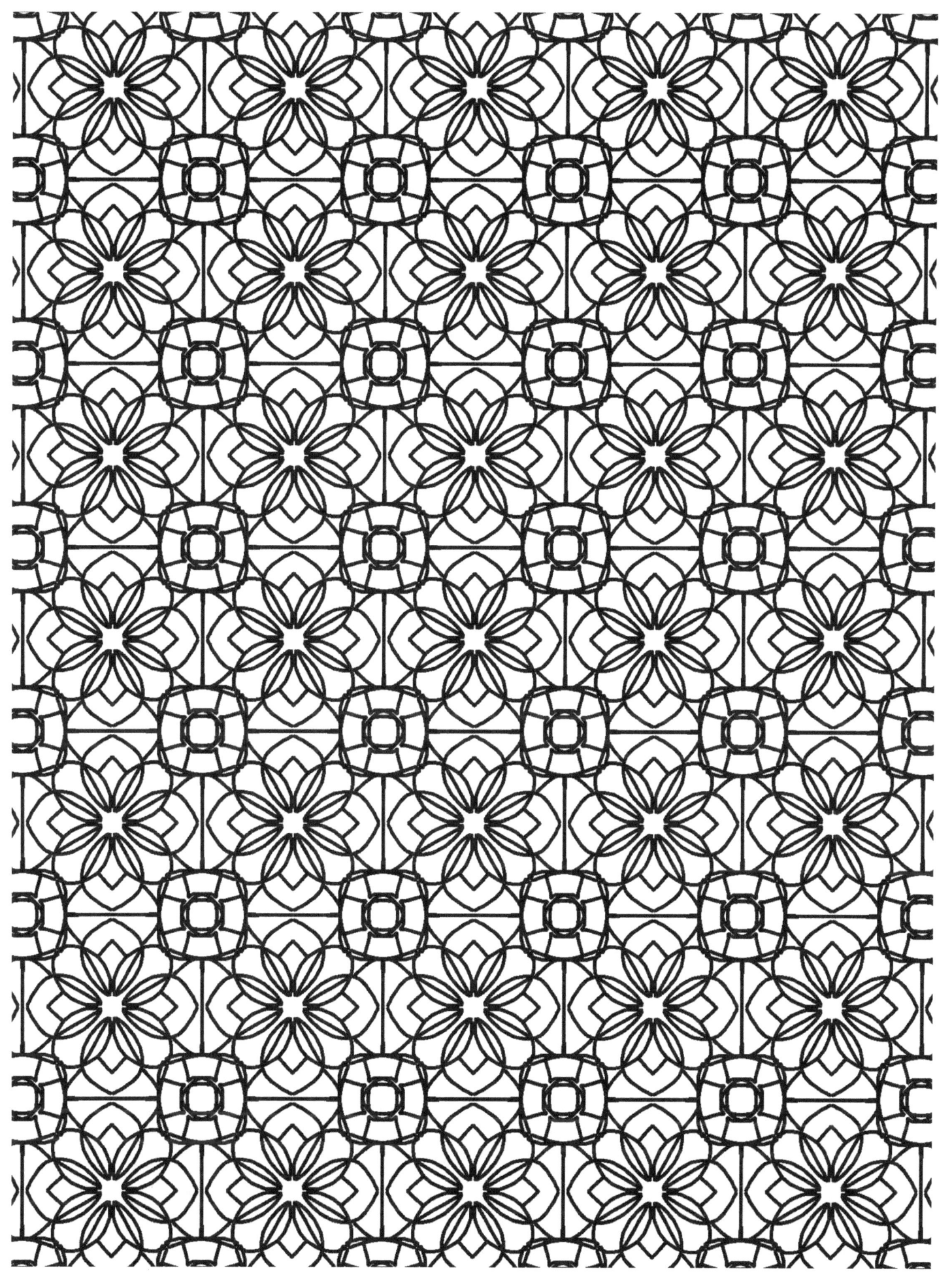

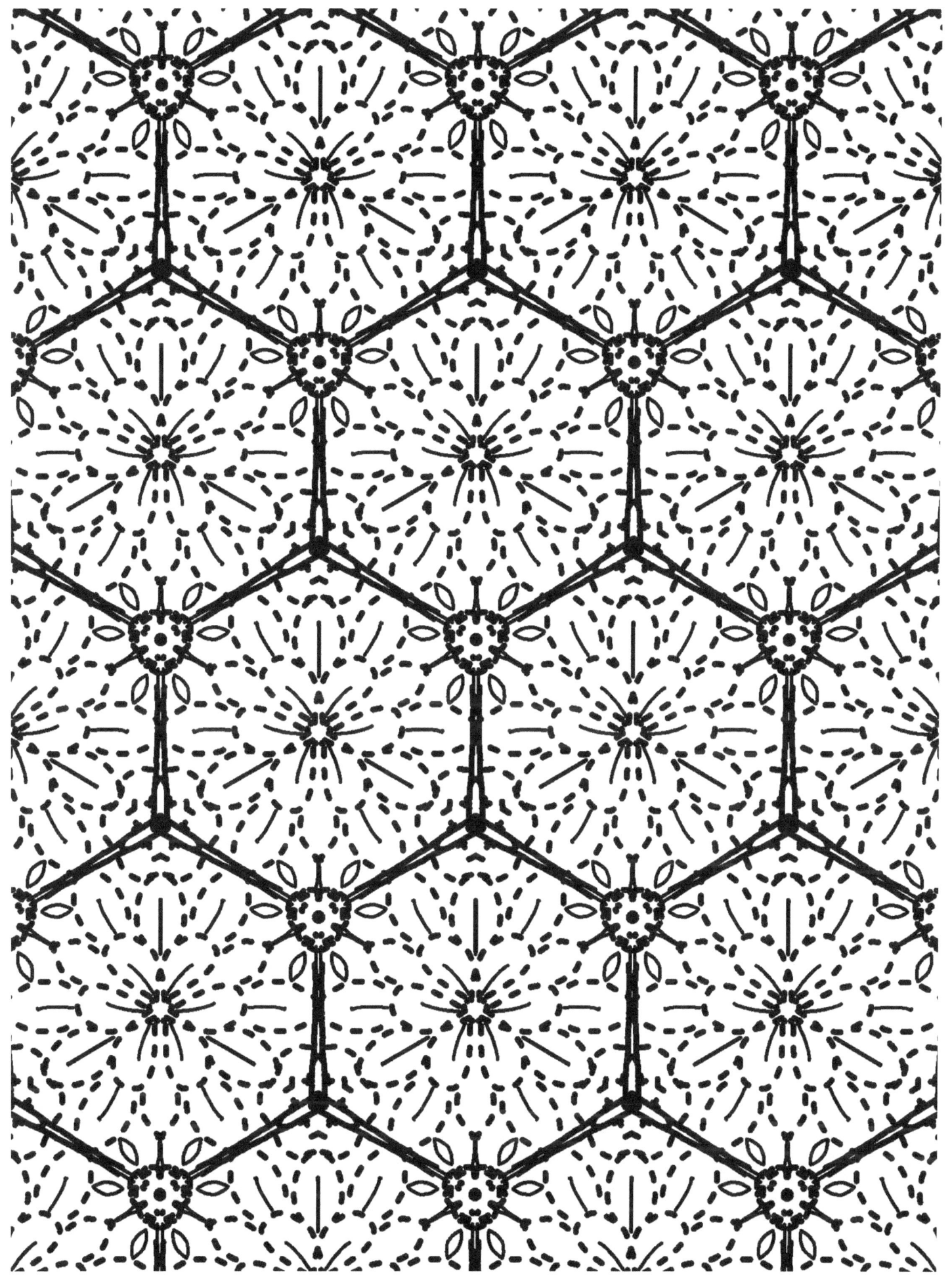

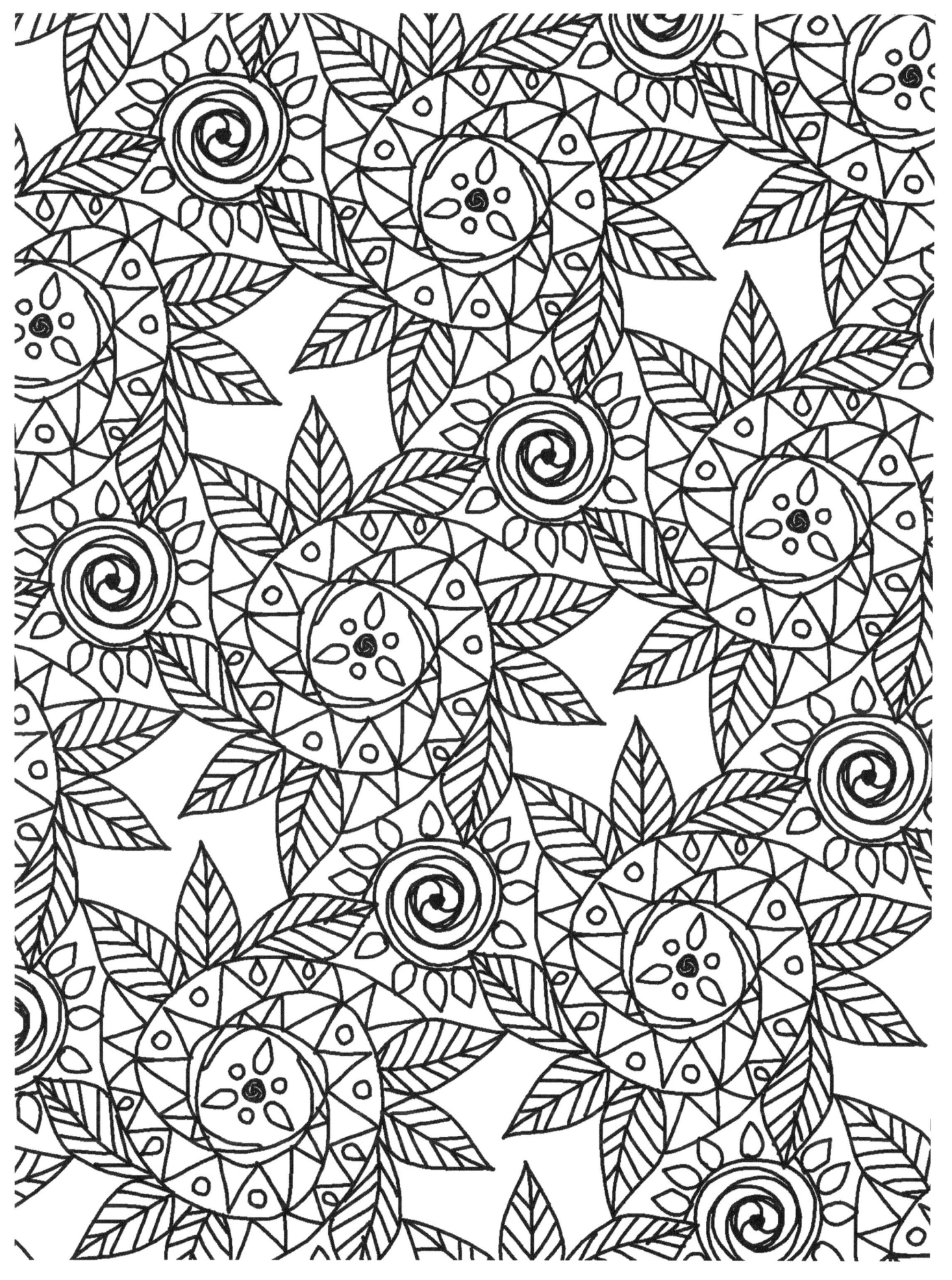

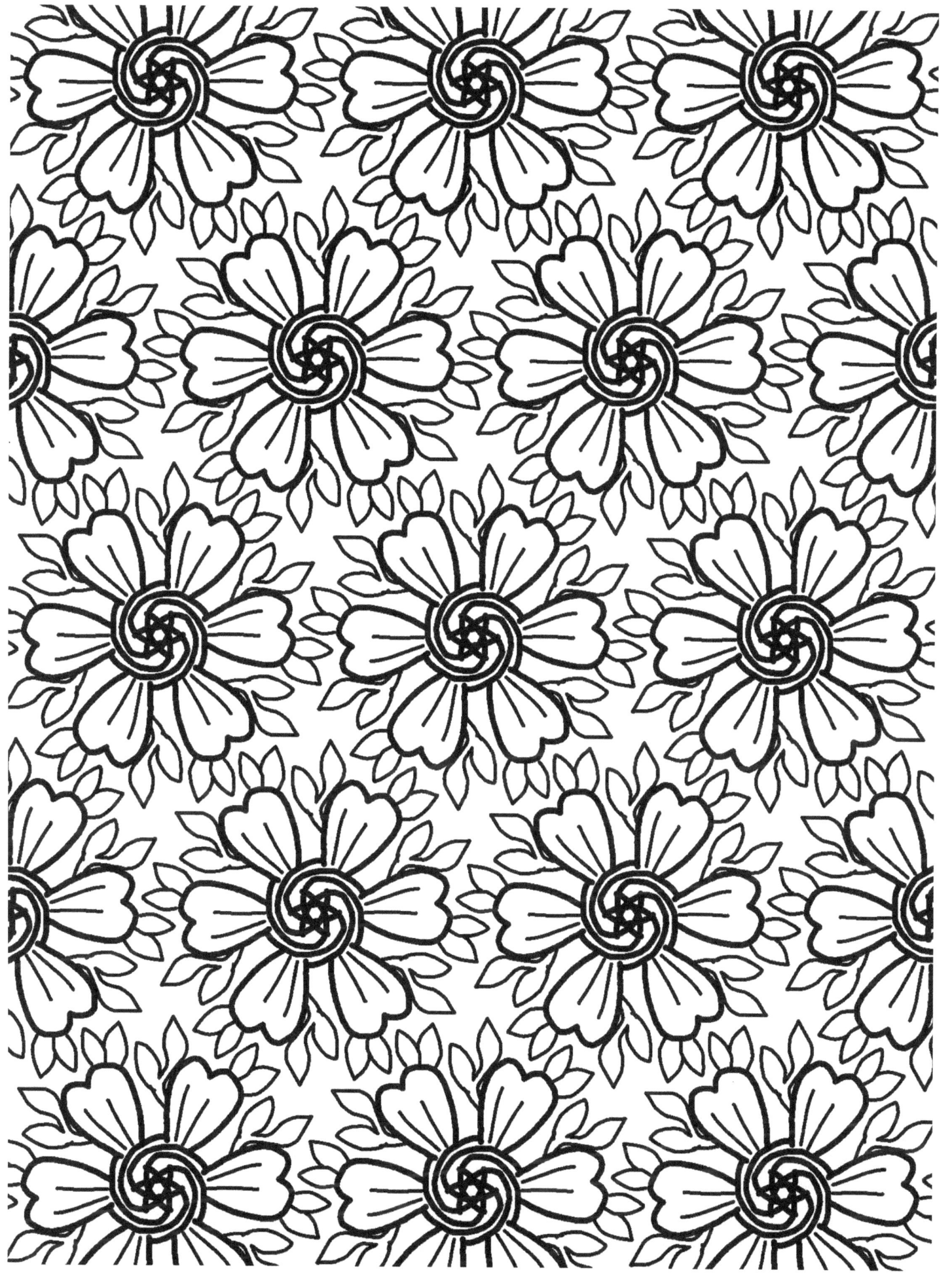

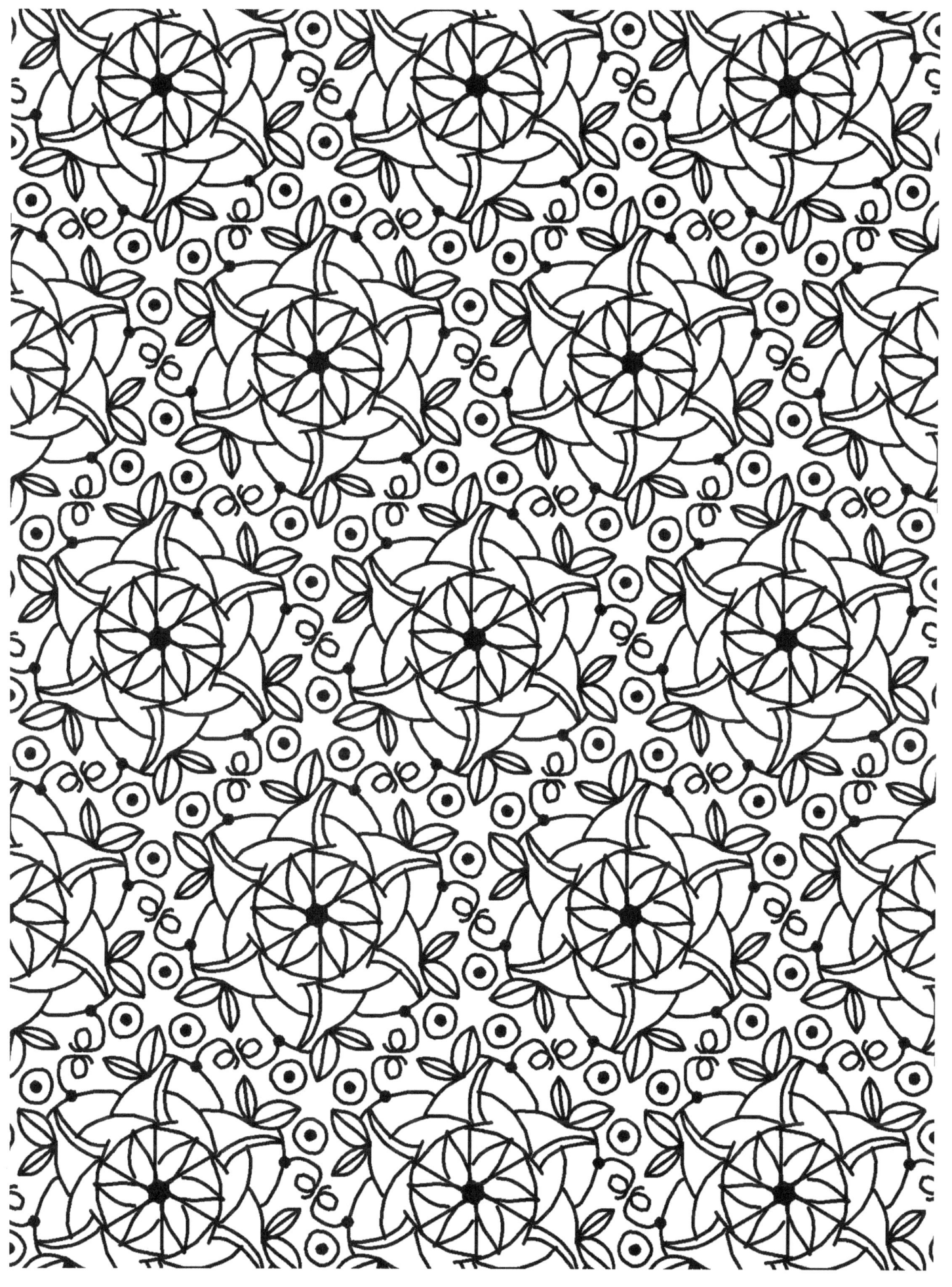

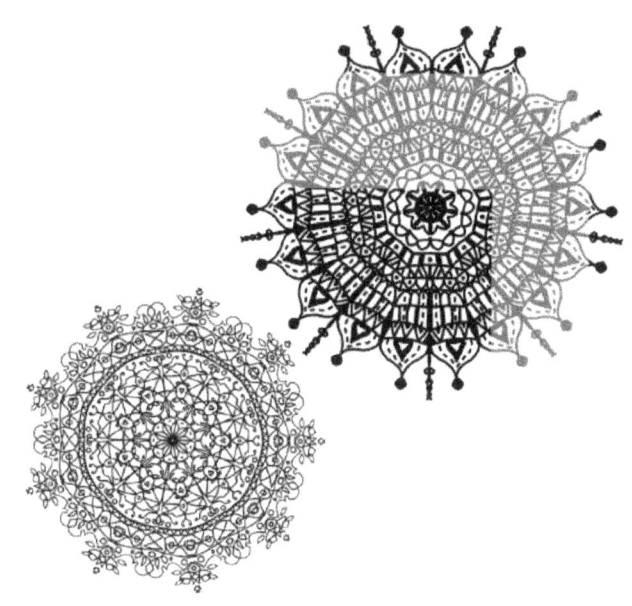

Mandala

Coloring can be a deeply calming and fulfilling creative activity. Free from the necessity of drawing, one can relax into the pleasure of filling space with color without having to do anything right- a meditative activity for anyone at any age. If you focus only on coloring them joyfully letting go of outside concerns, you can be brought to a quite state of mind

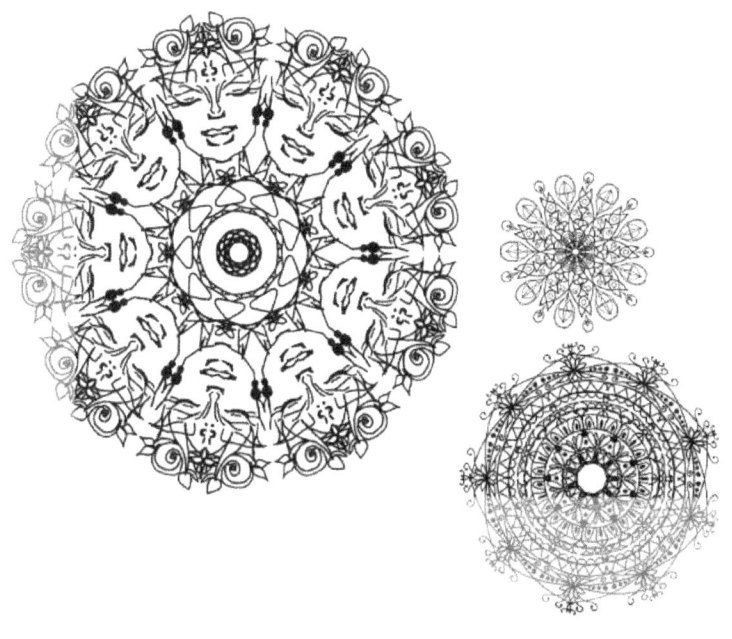

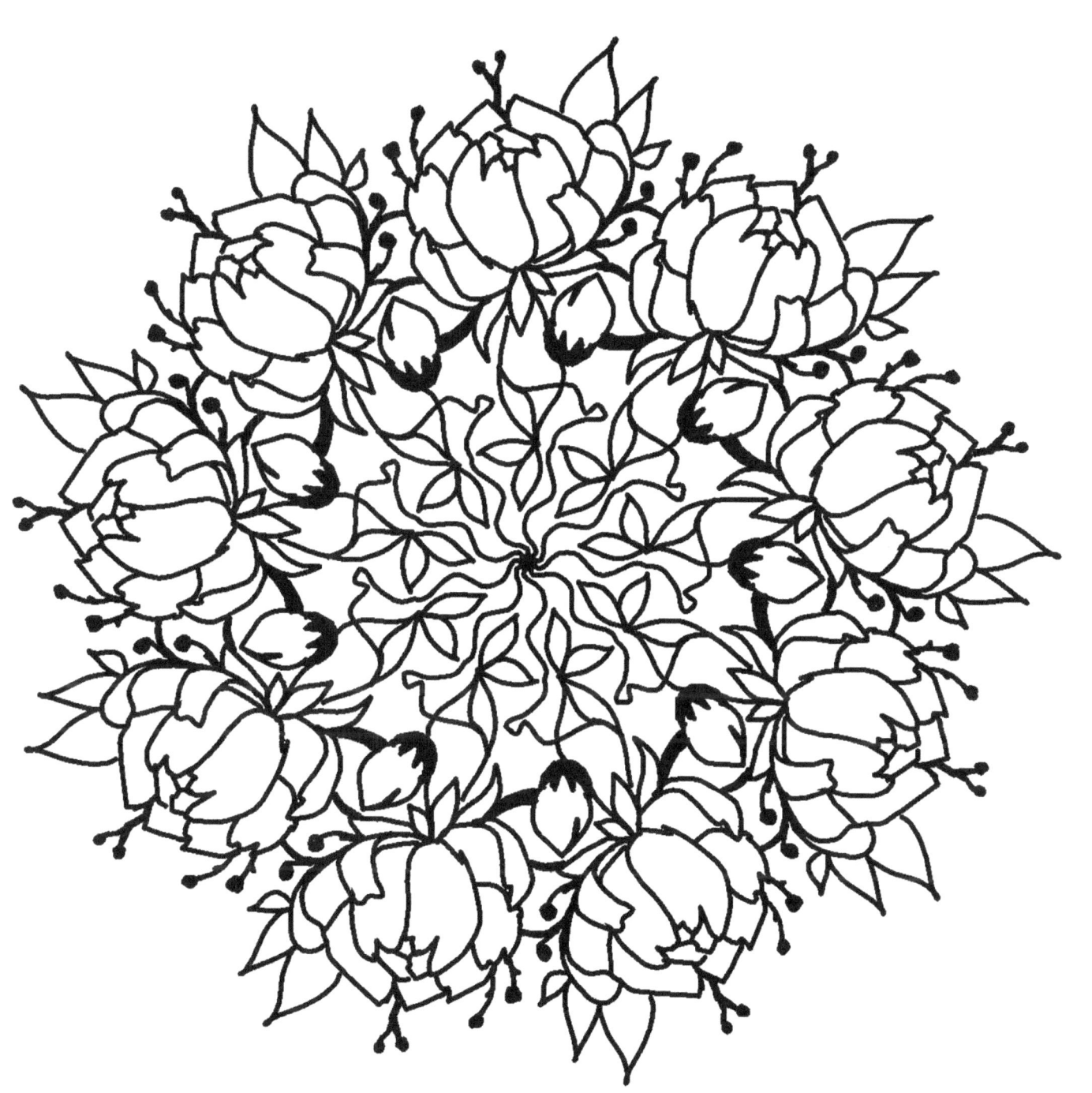

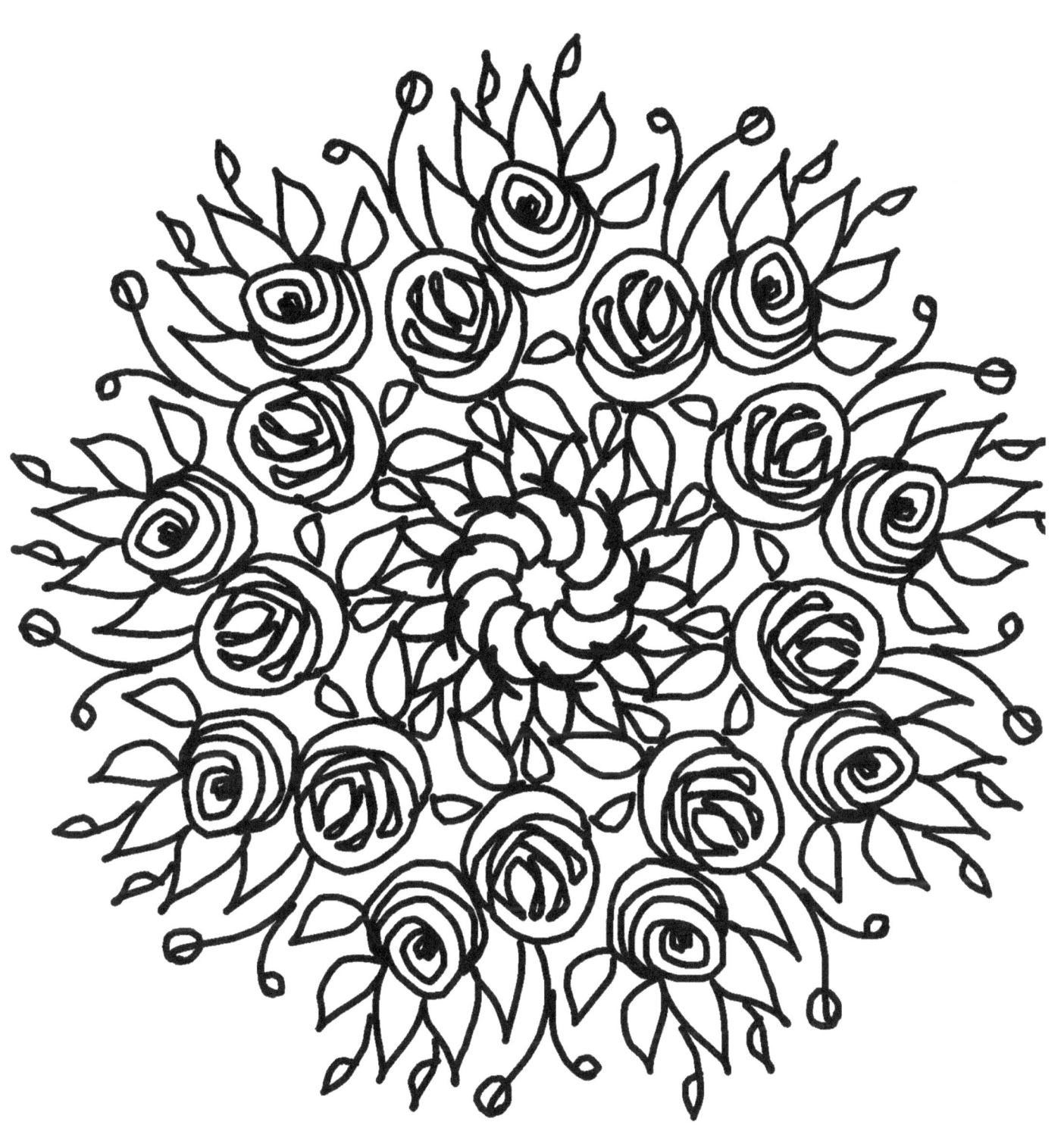

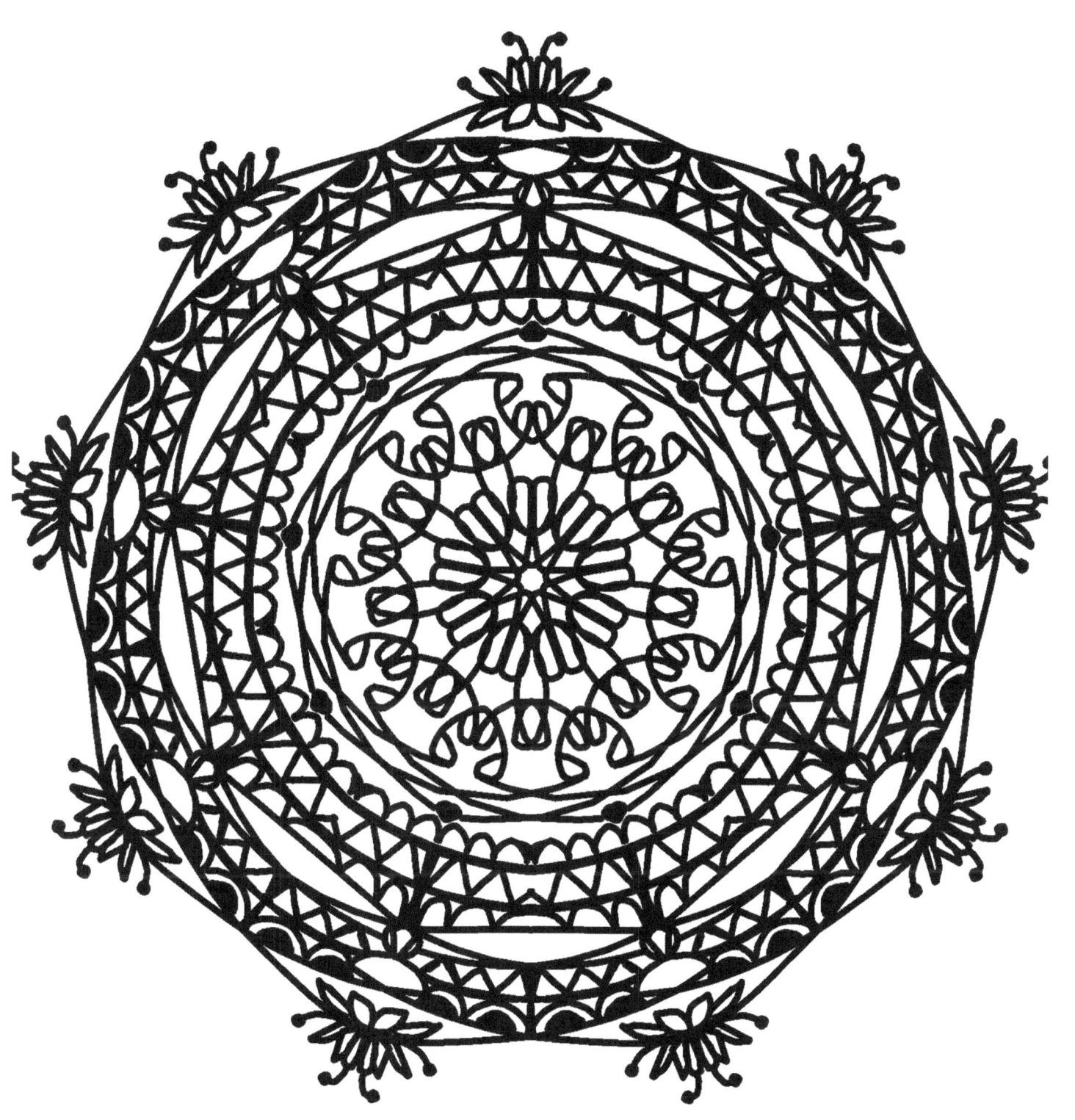

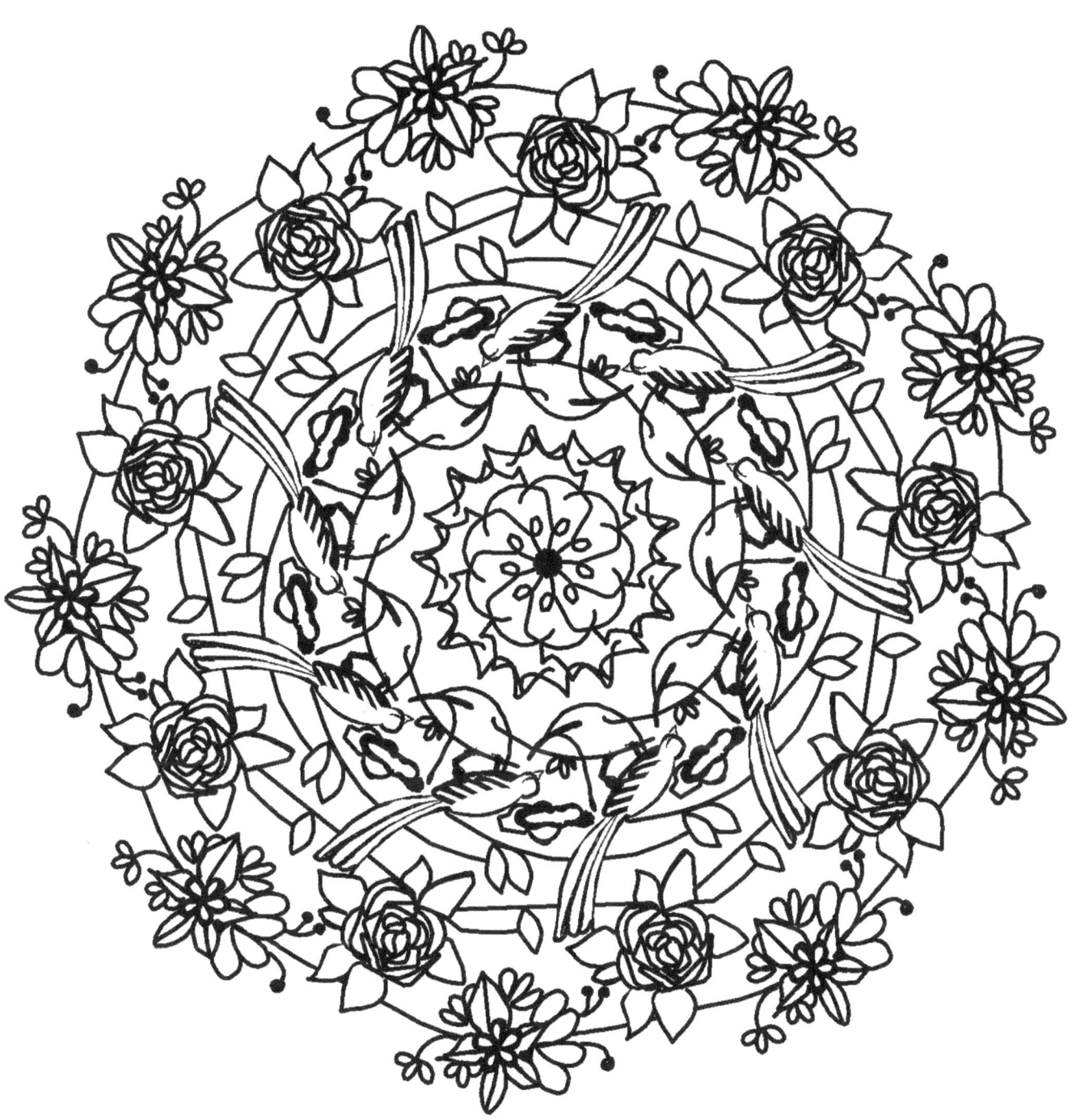

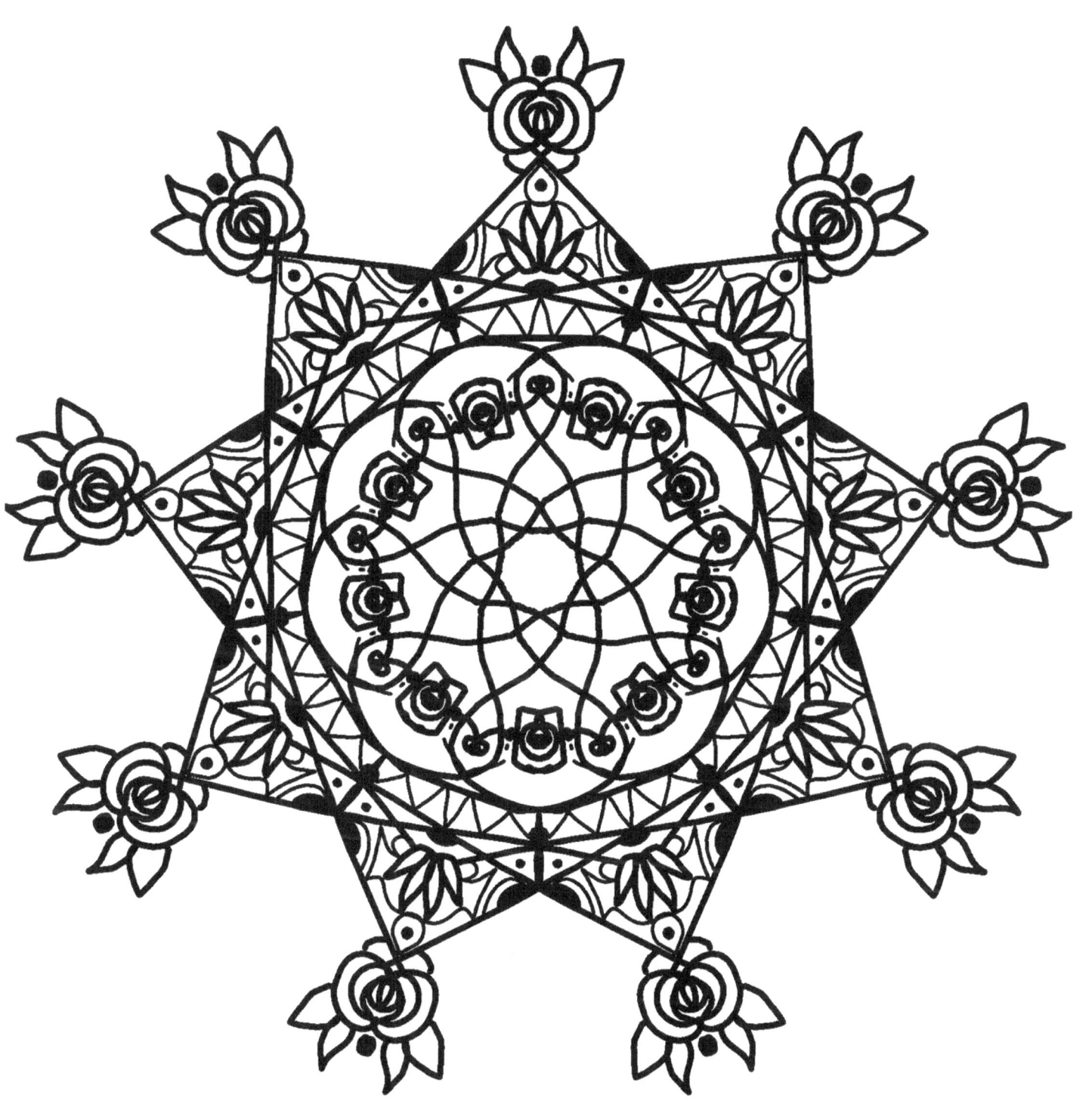

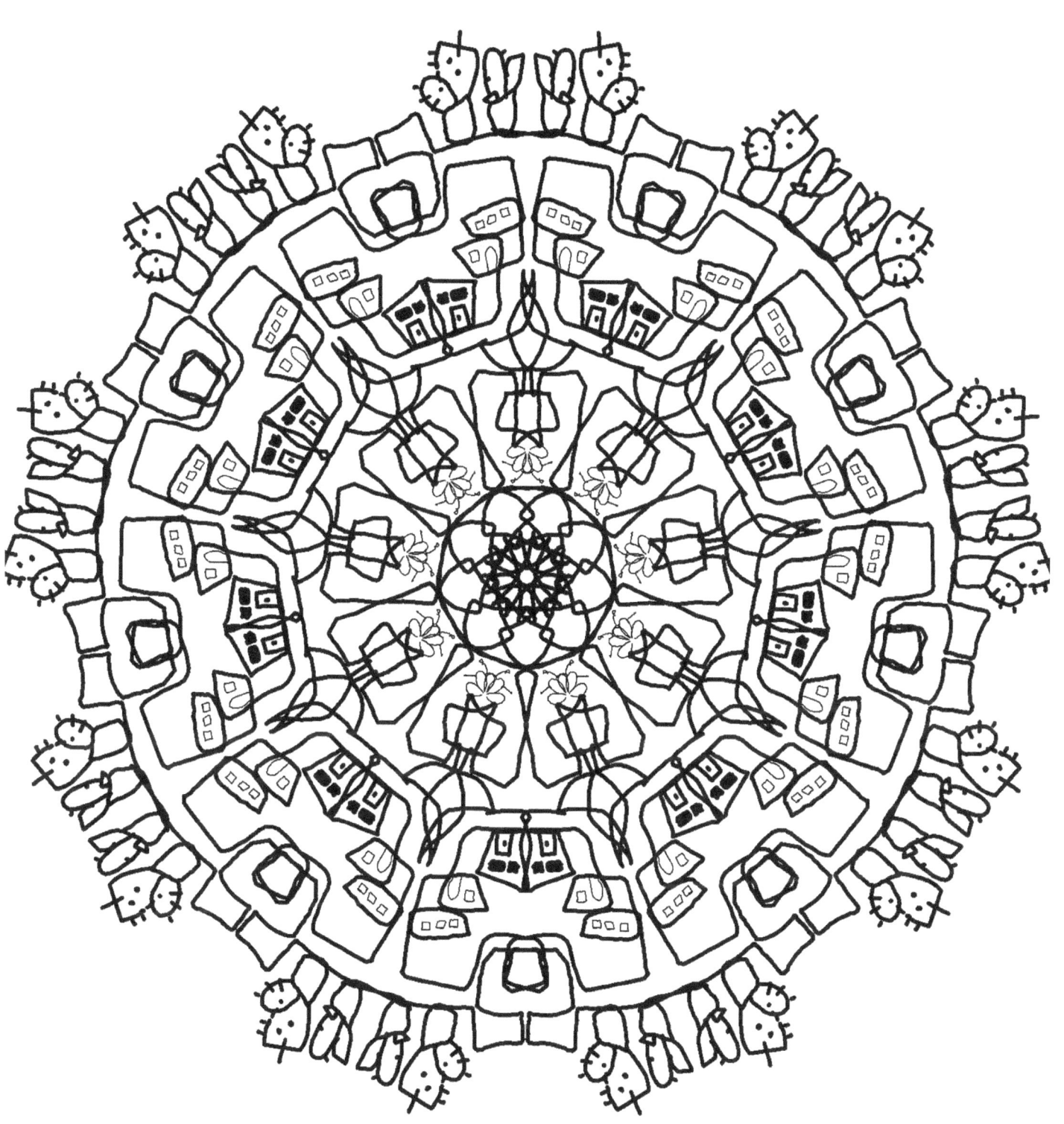

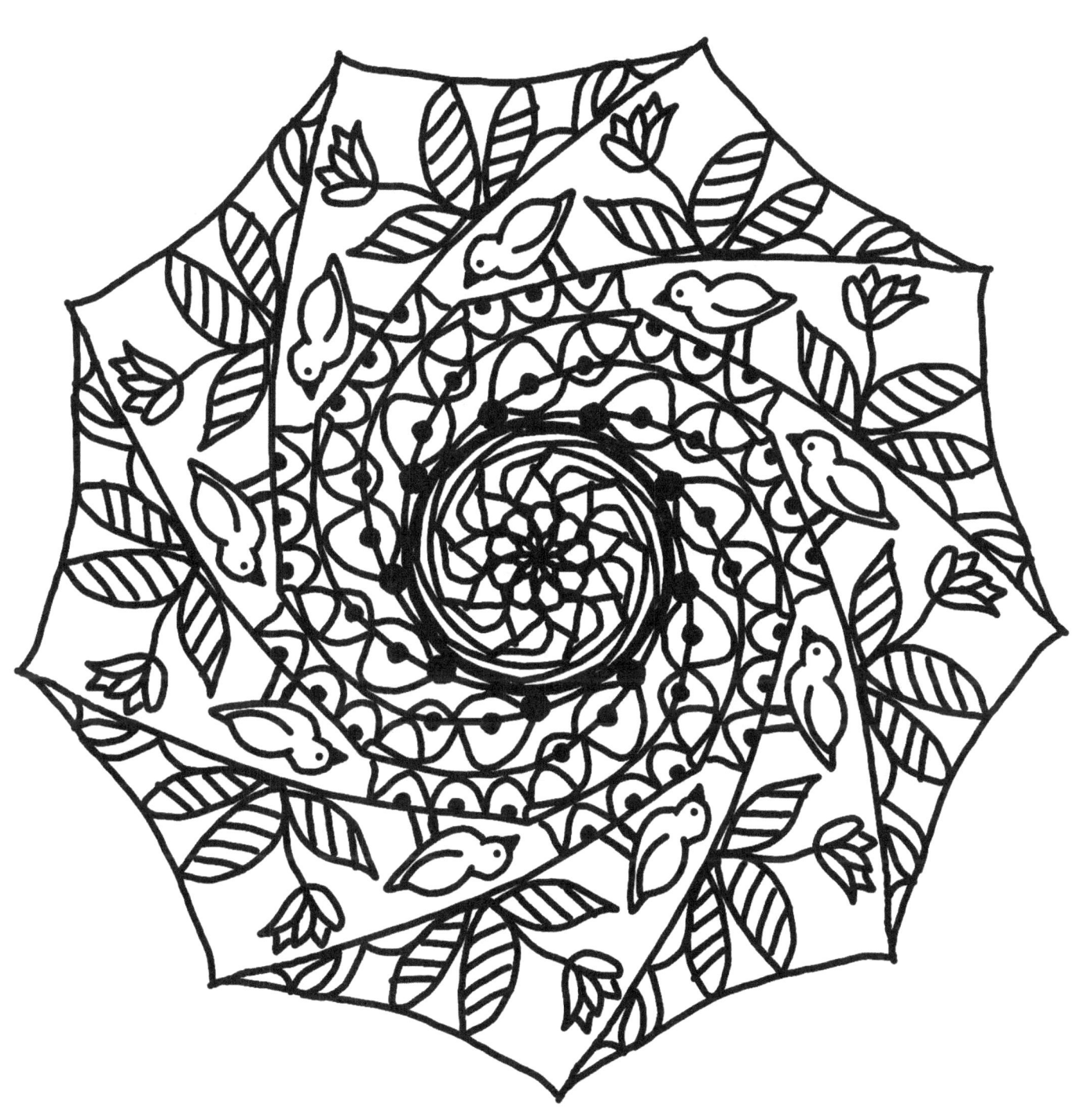

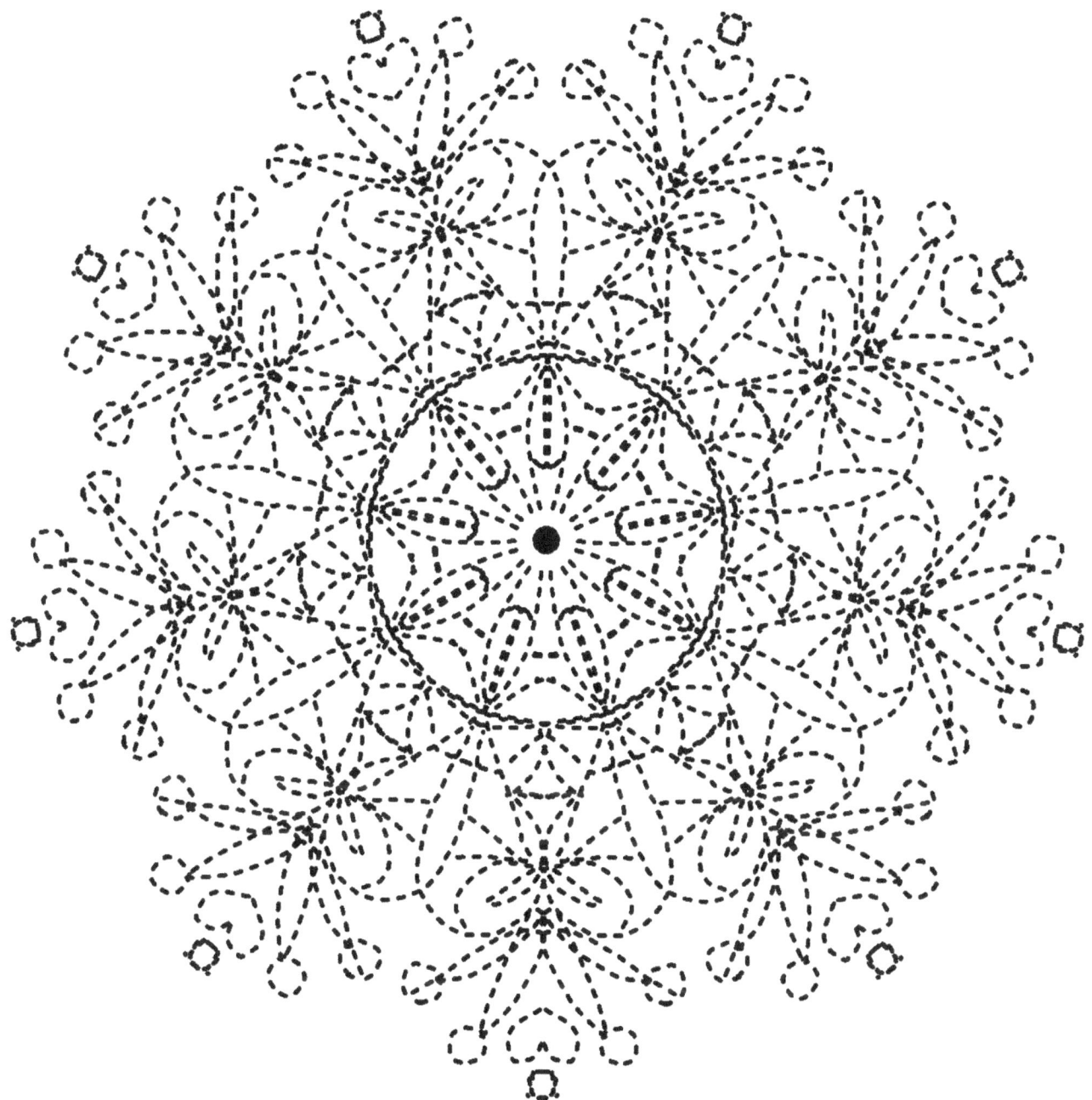

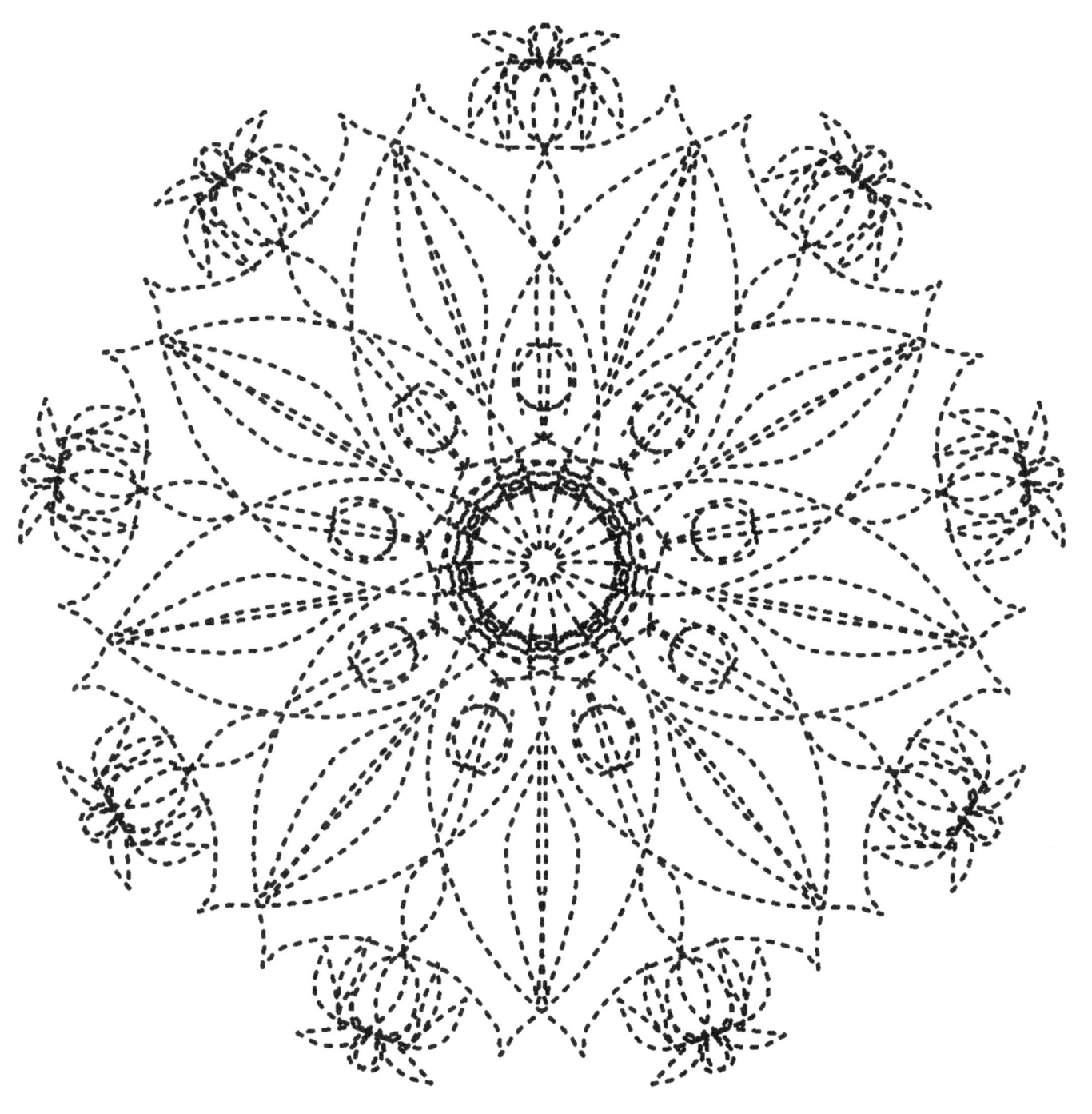

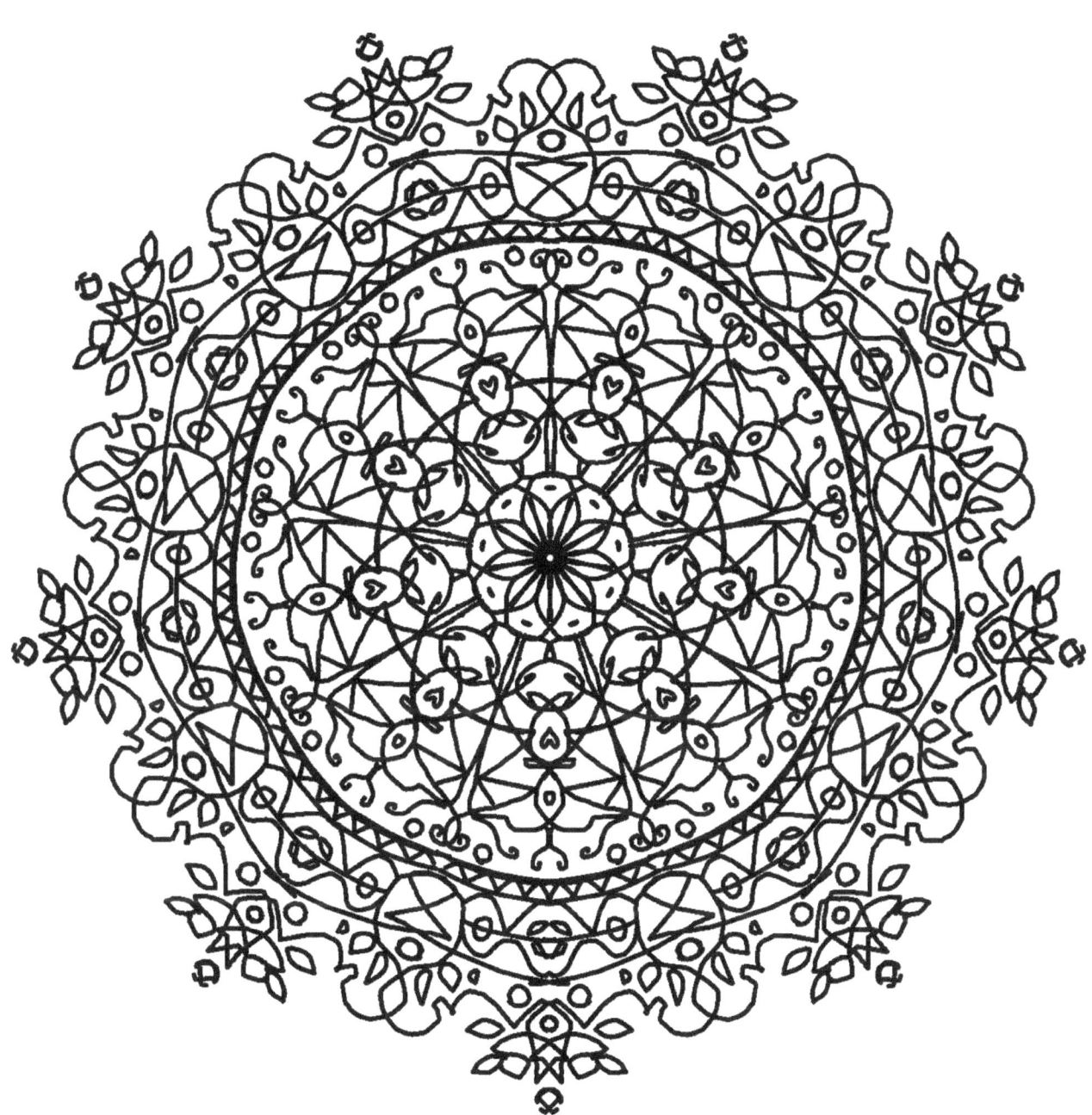

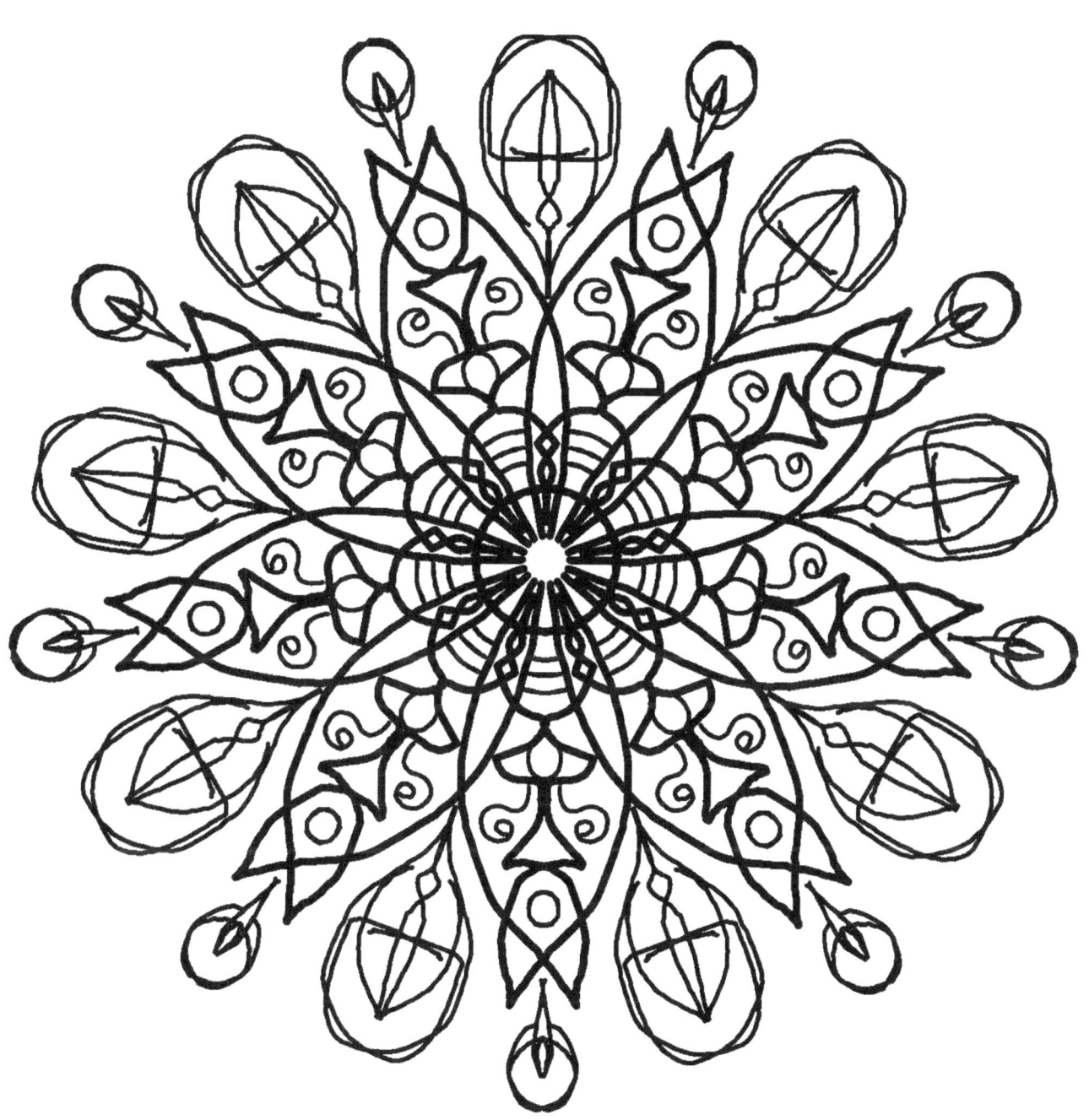

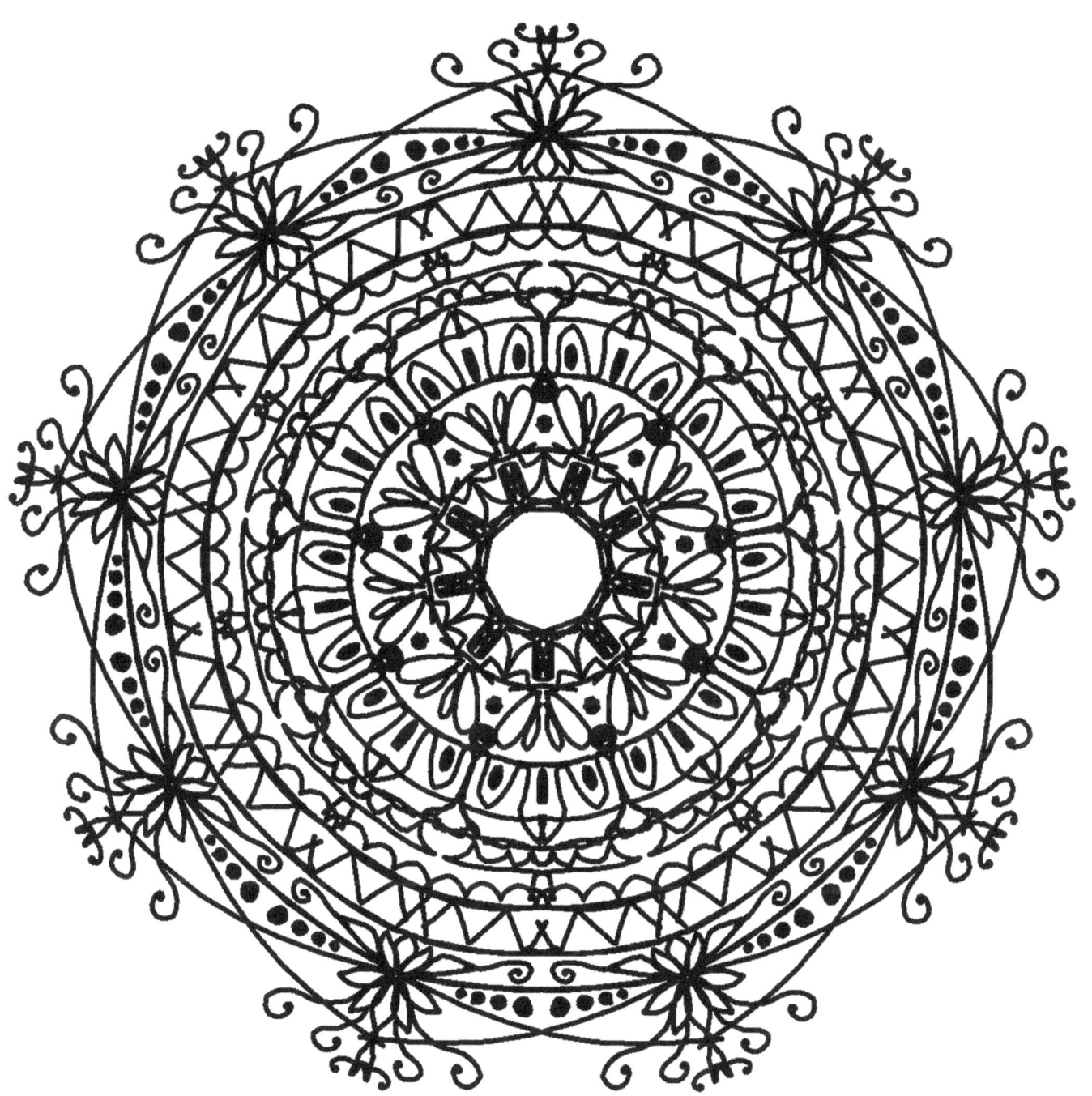

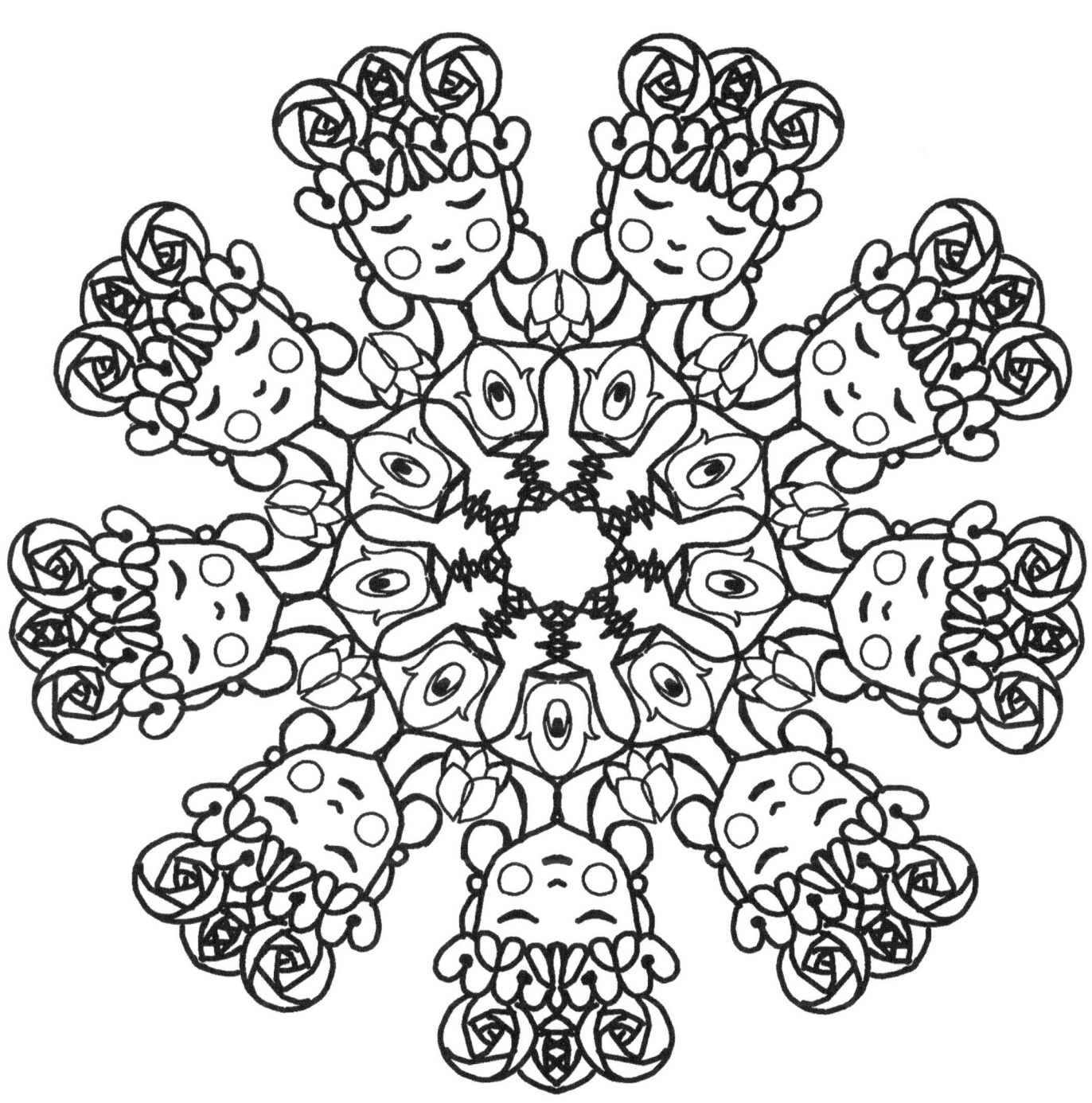

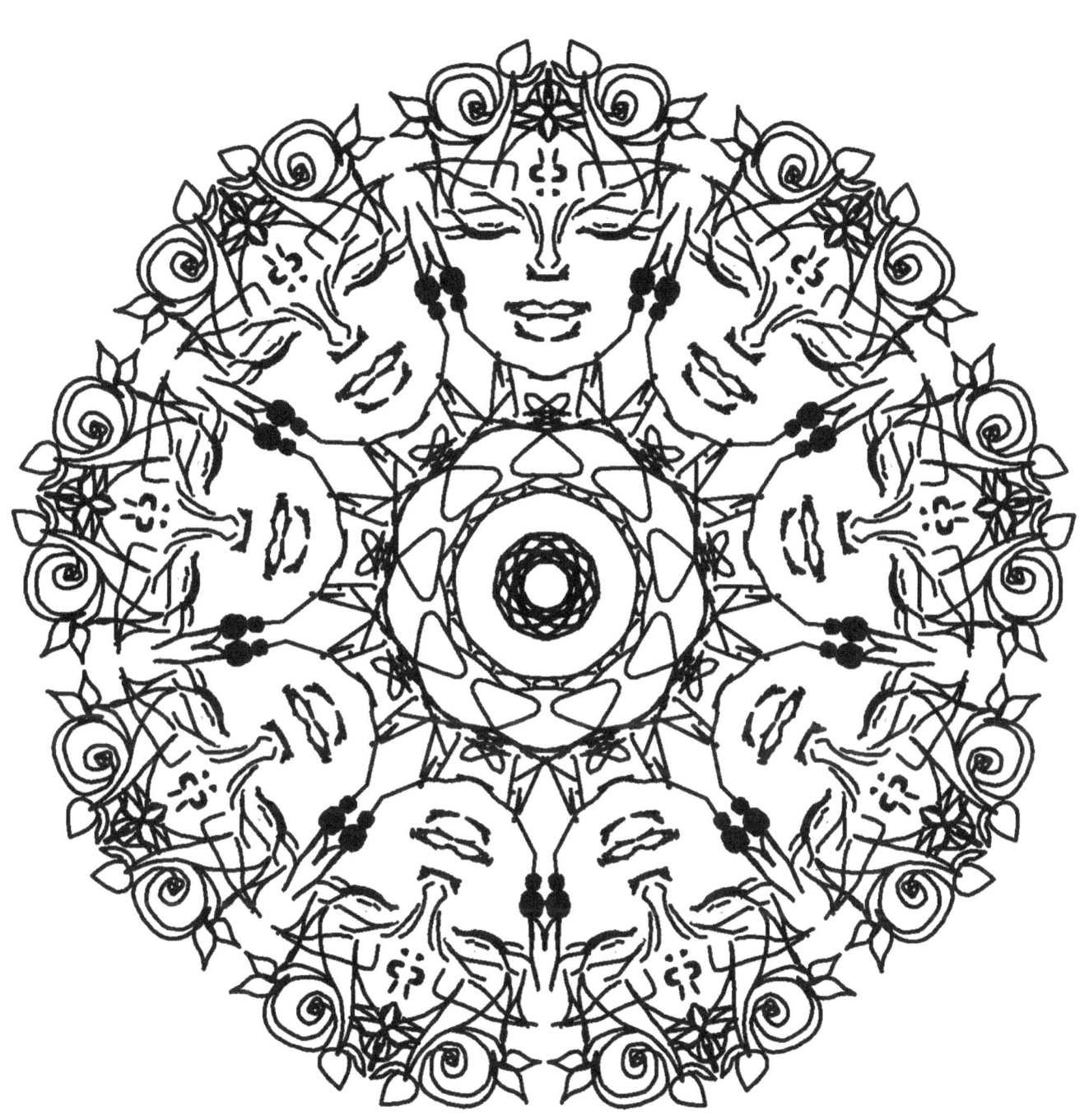

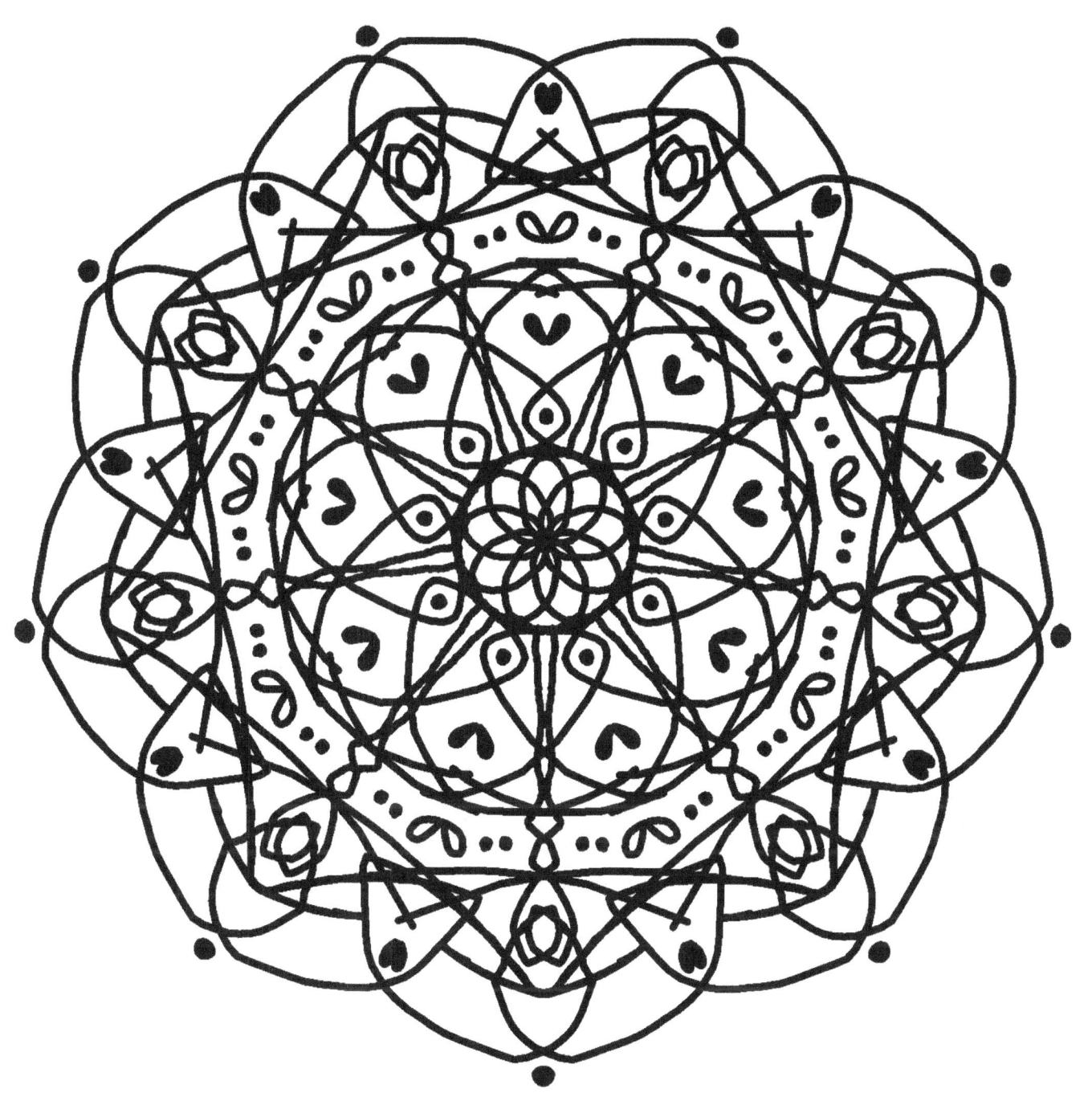

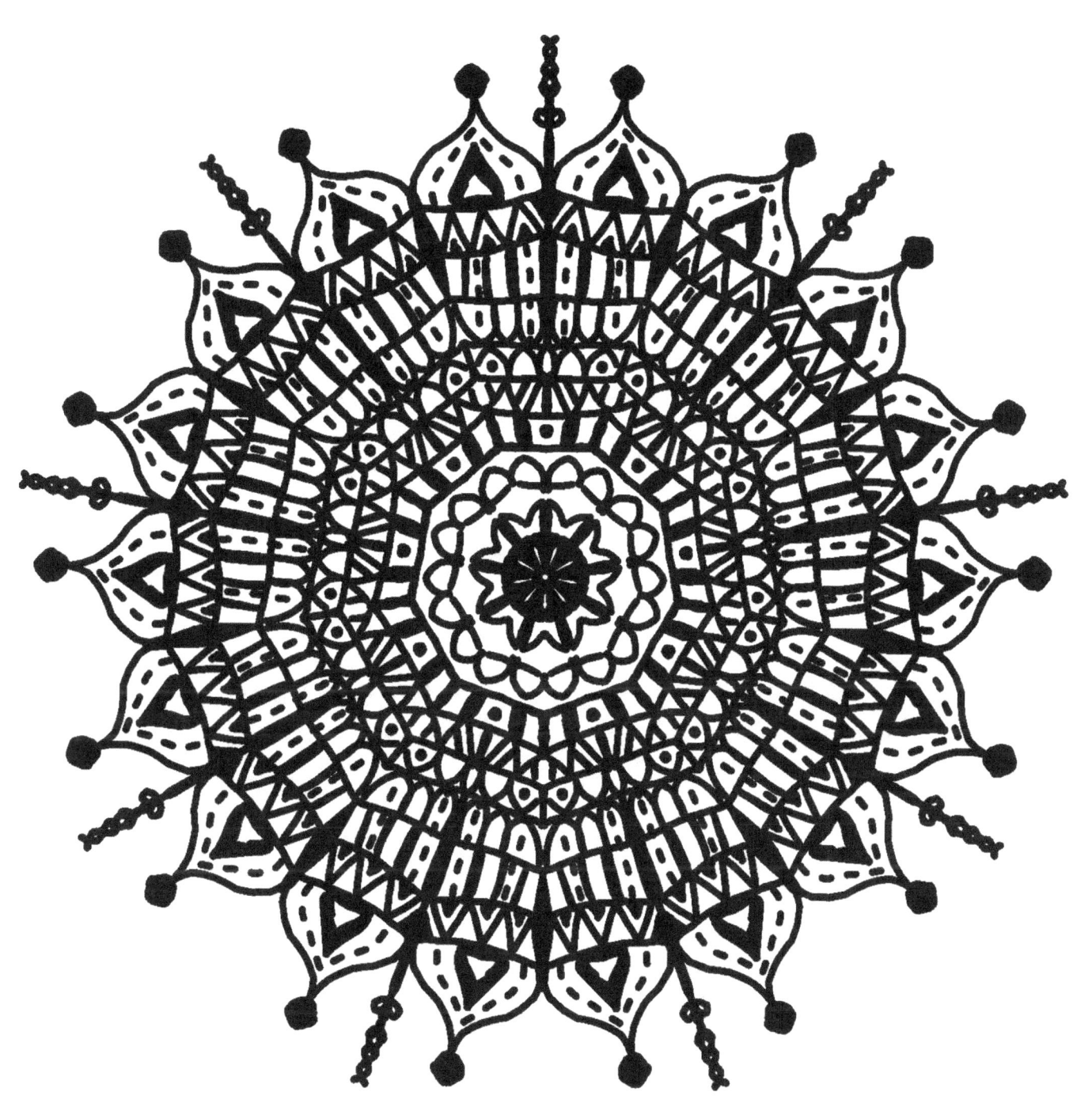

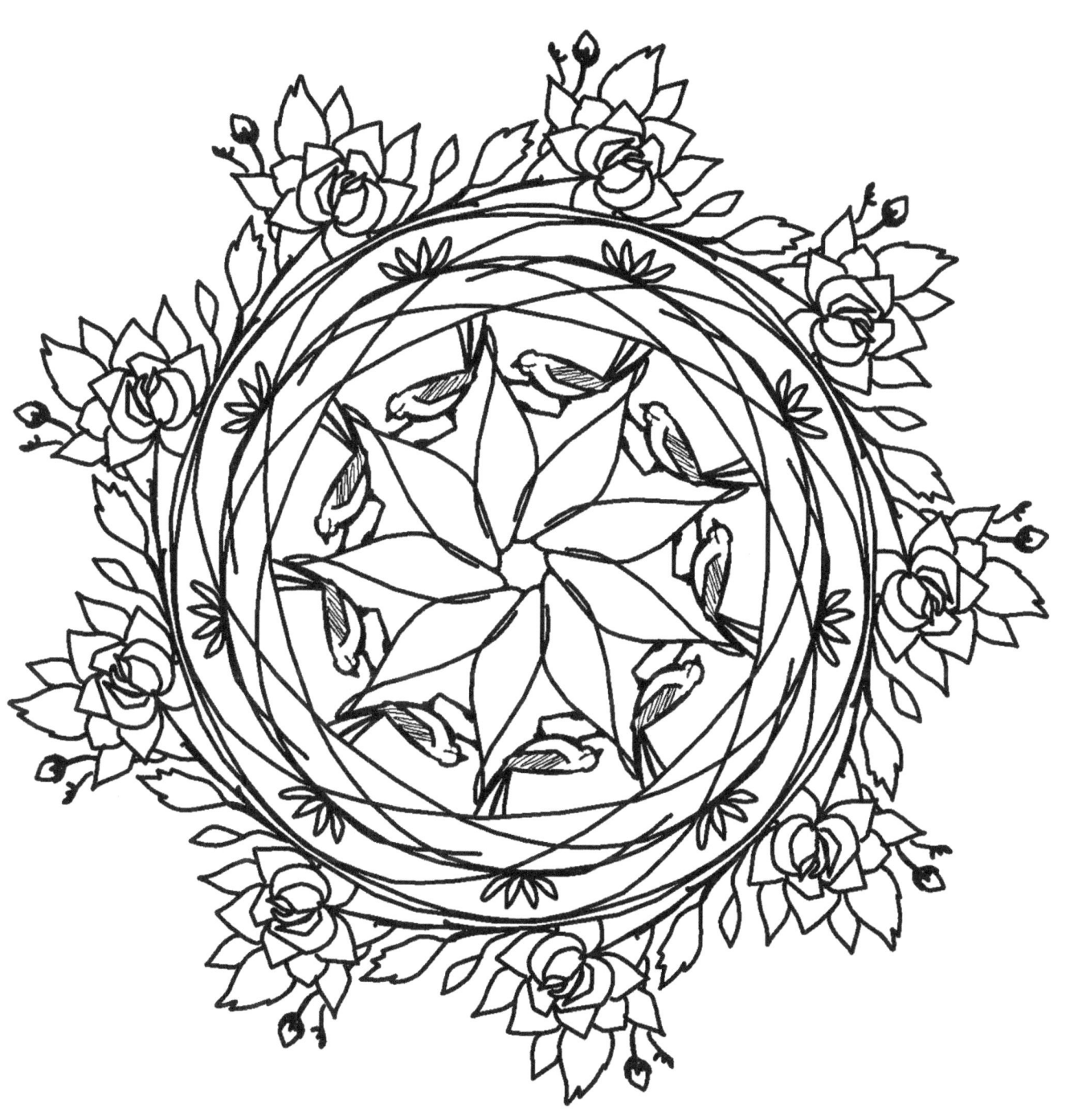

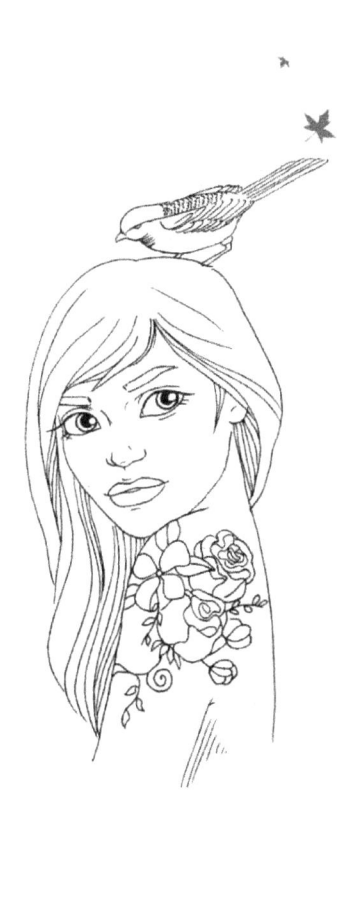

Relax, renew and

rejuvenate! Enjoy

yourself coloring these

18 original, hand drawn

feminine and floral

illustrations inspired by

nature's beauty and

tattoo designs.

Be yourself!

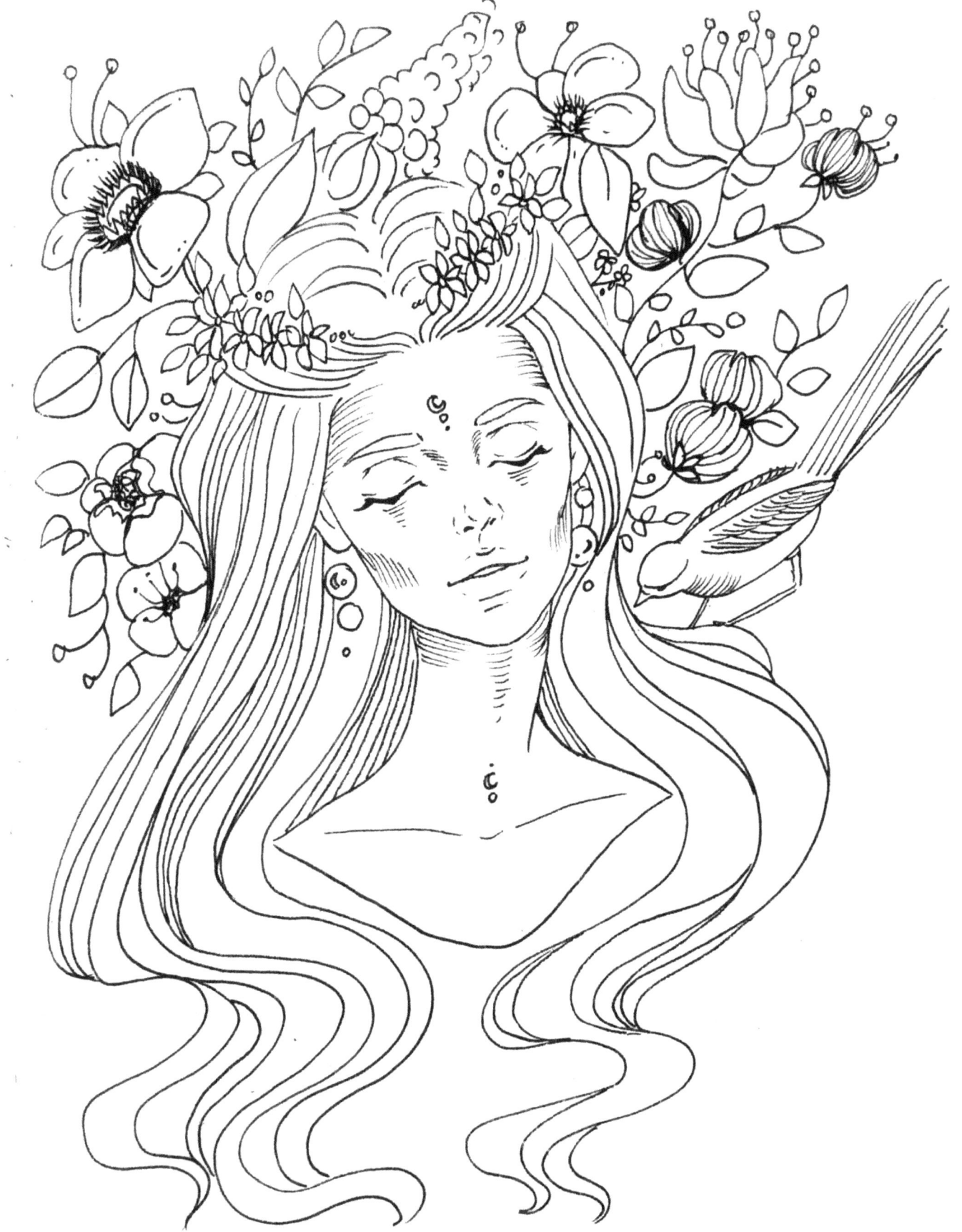

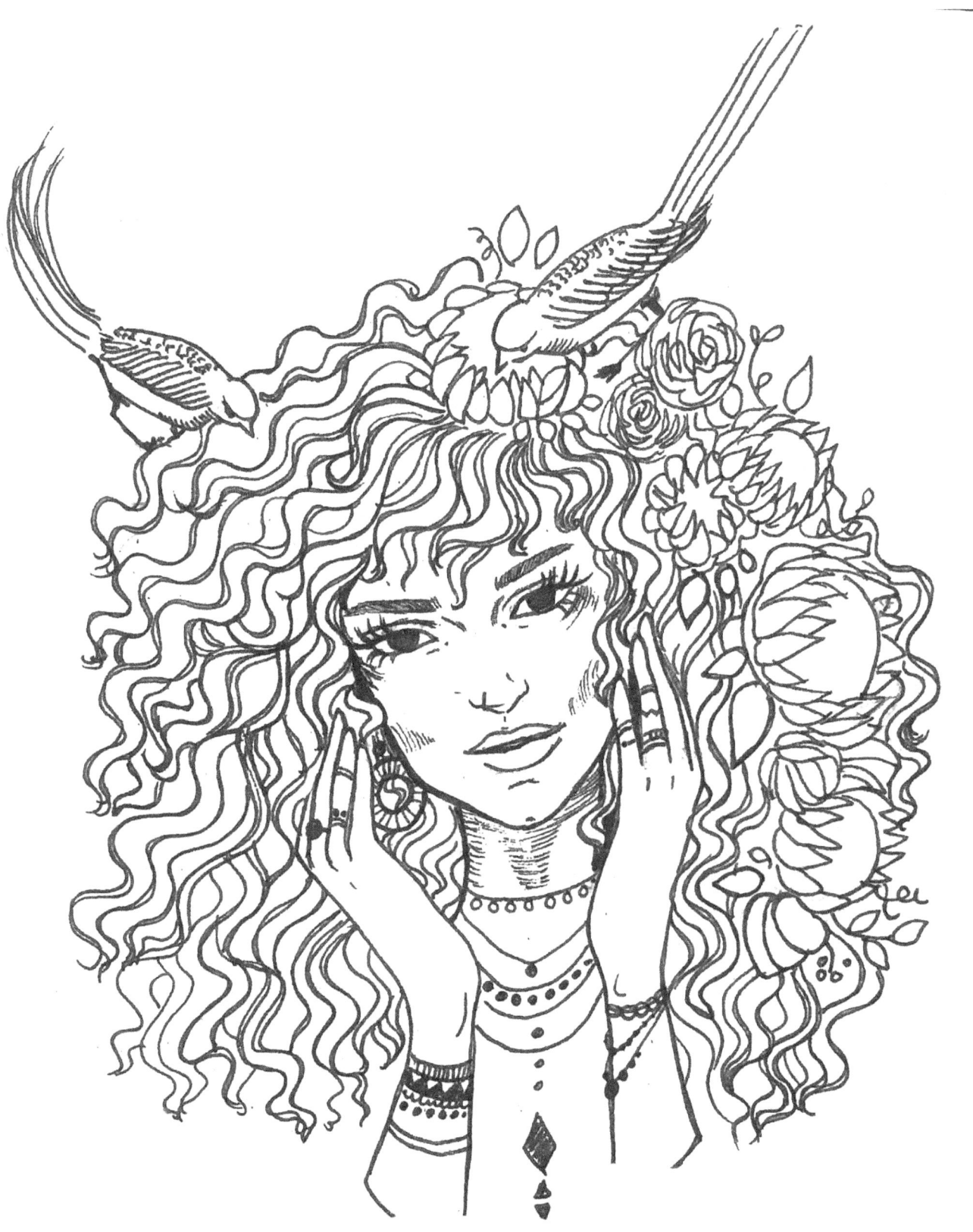

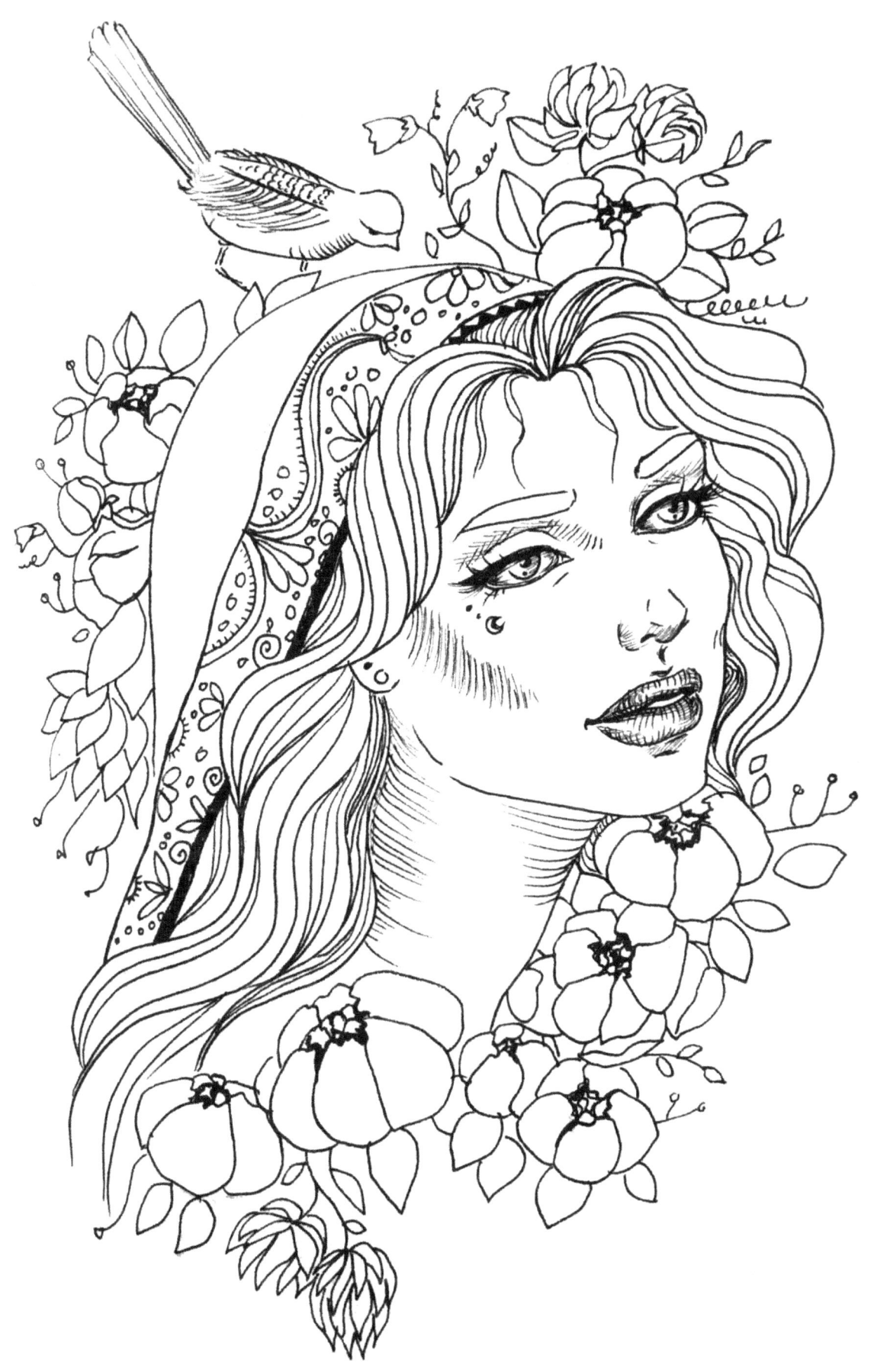

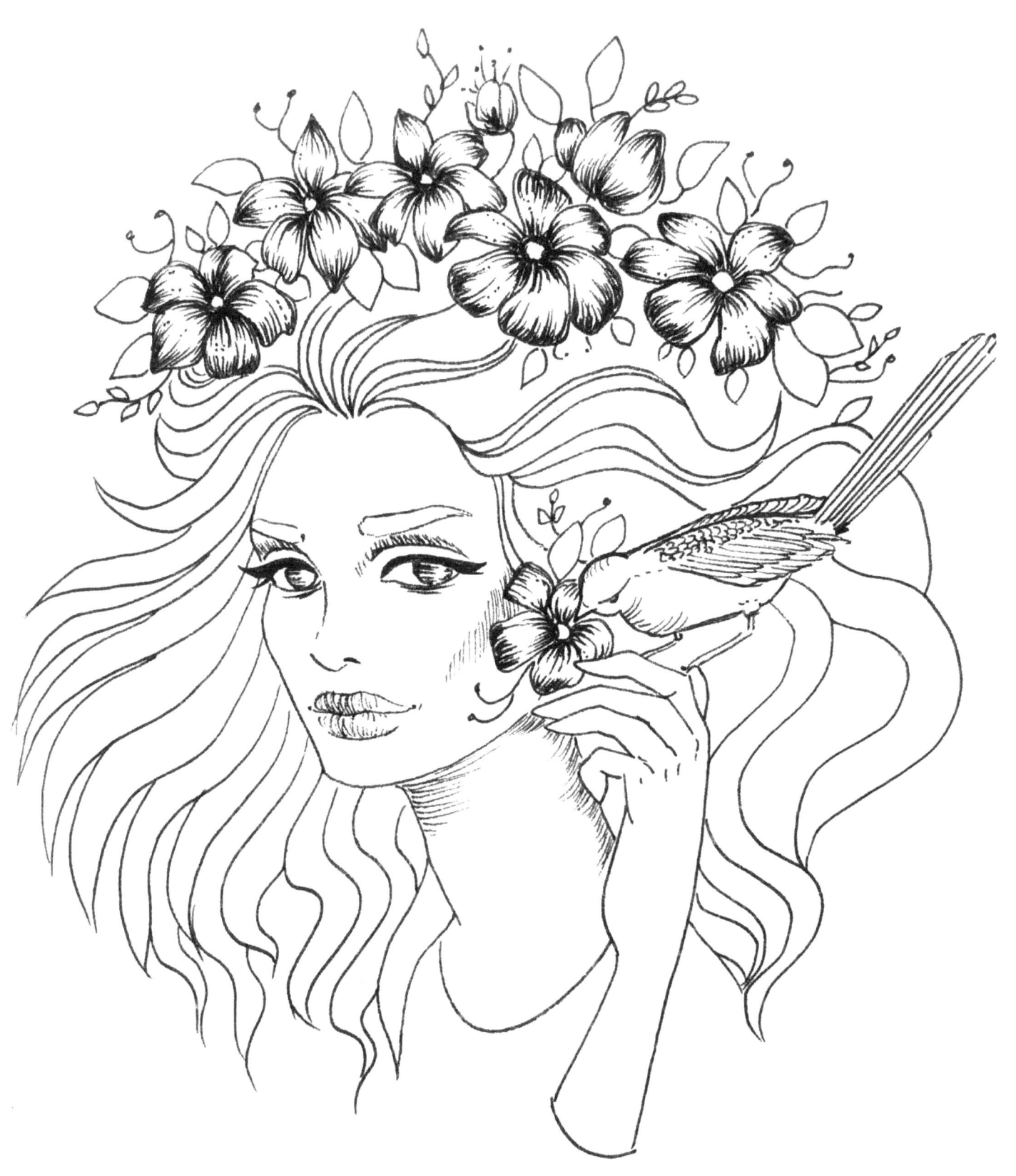

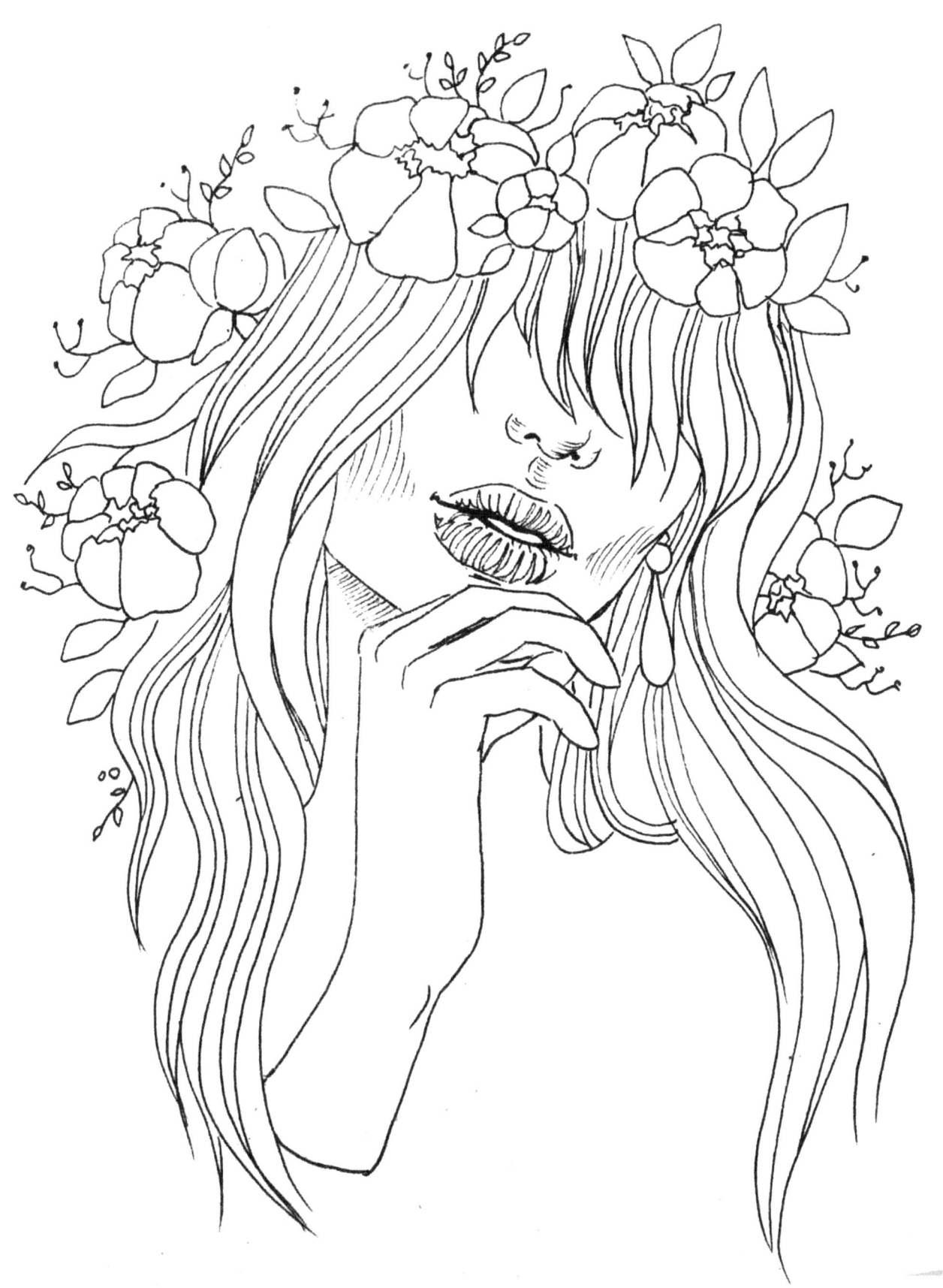

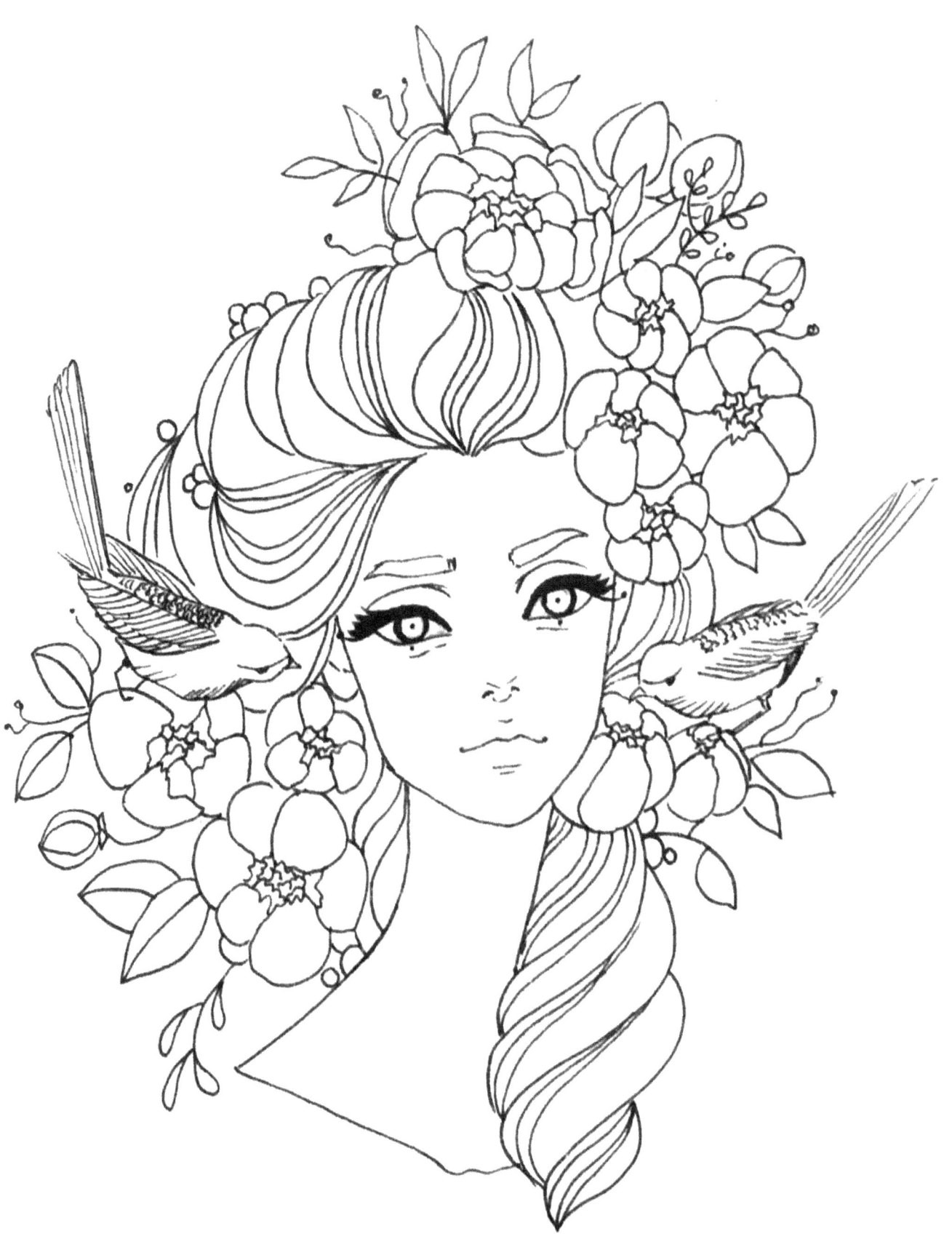

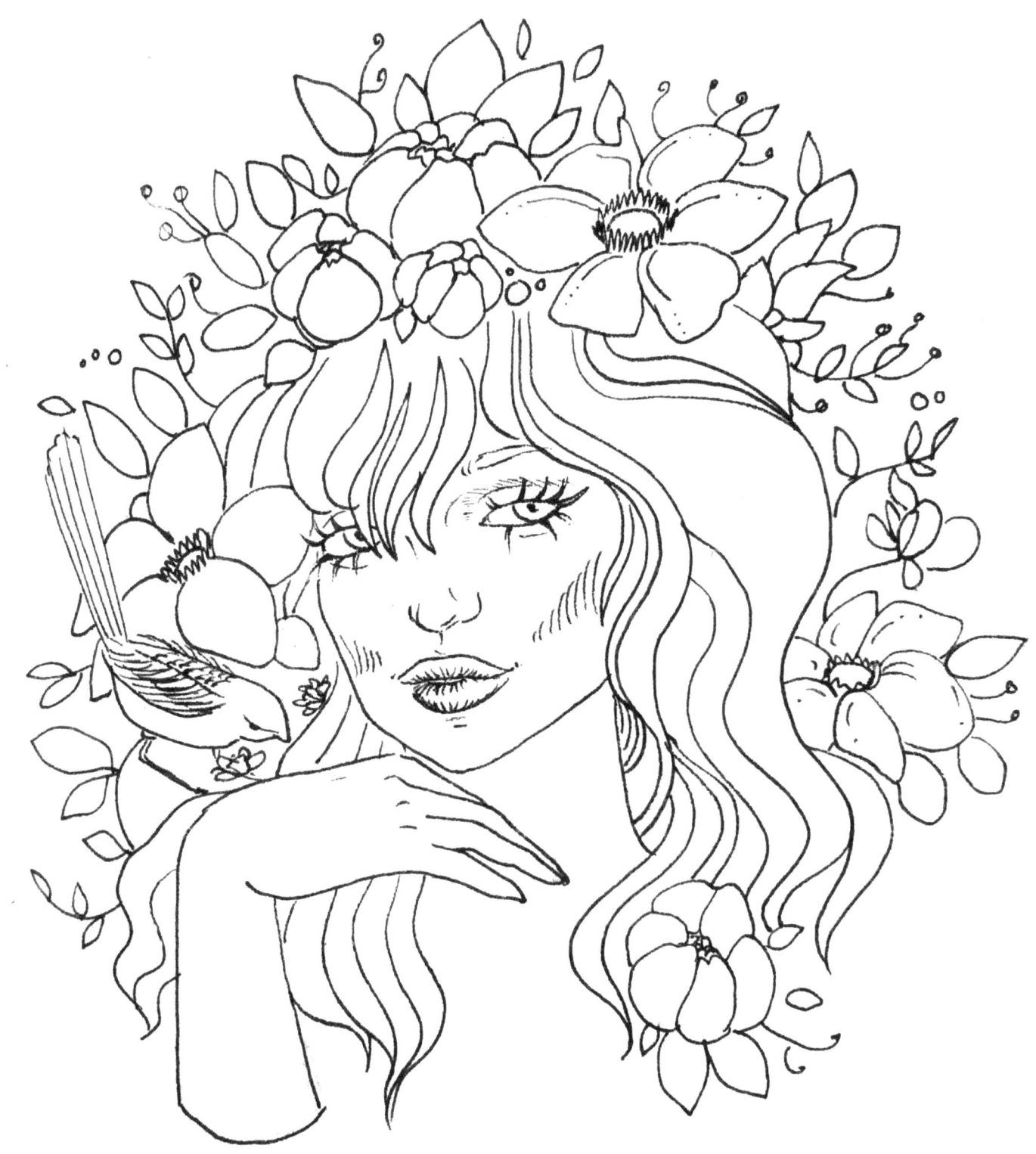

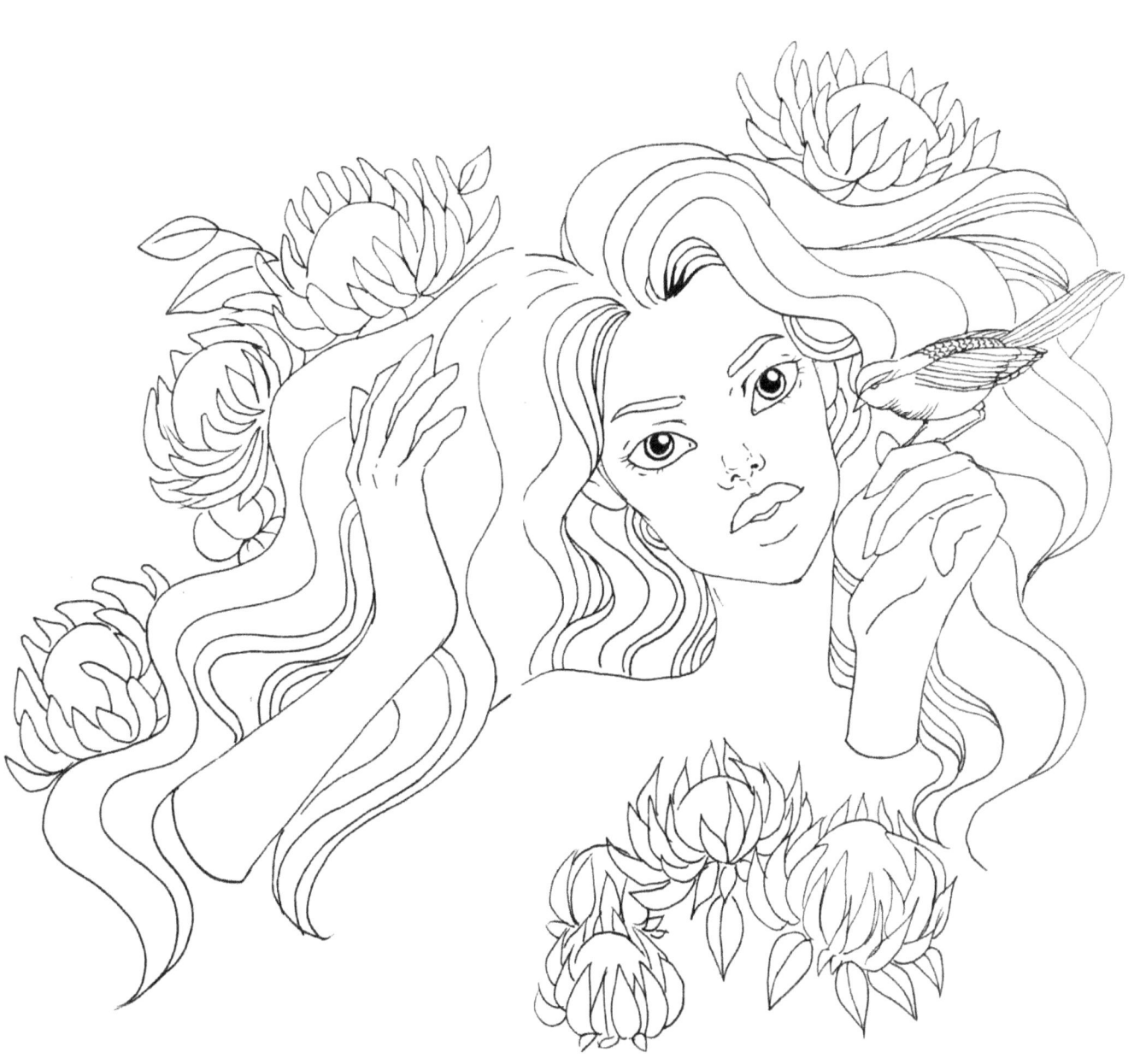

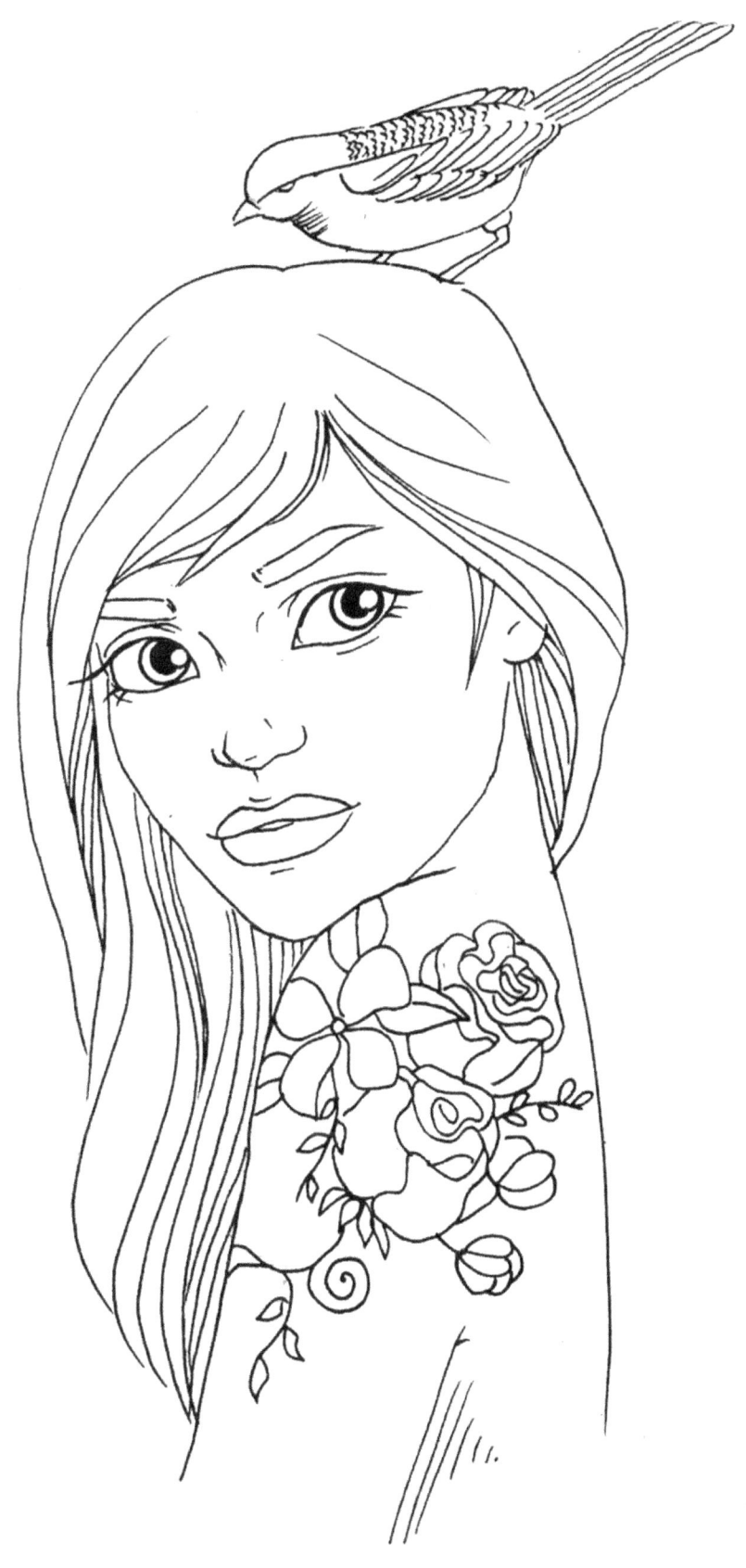

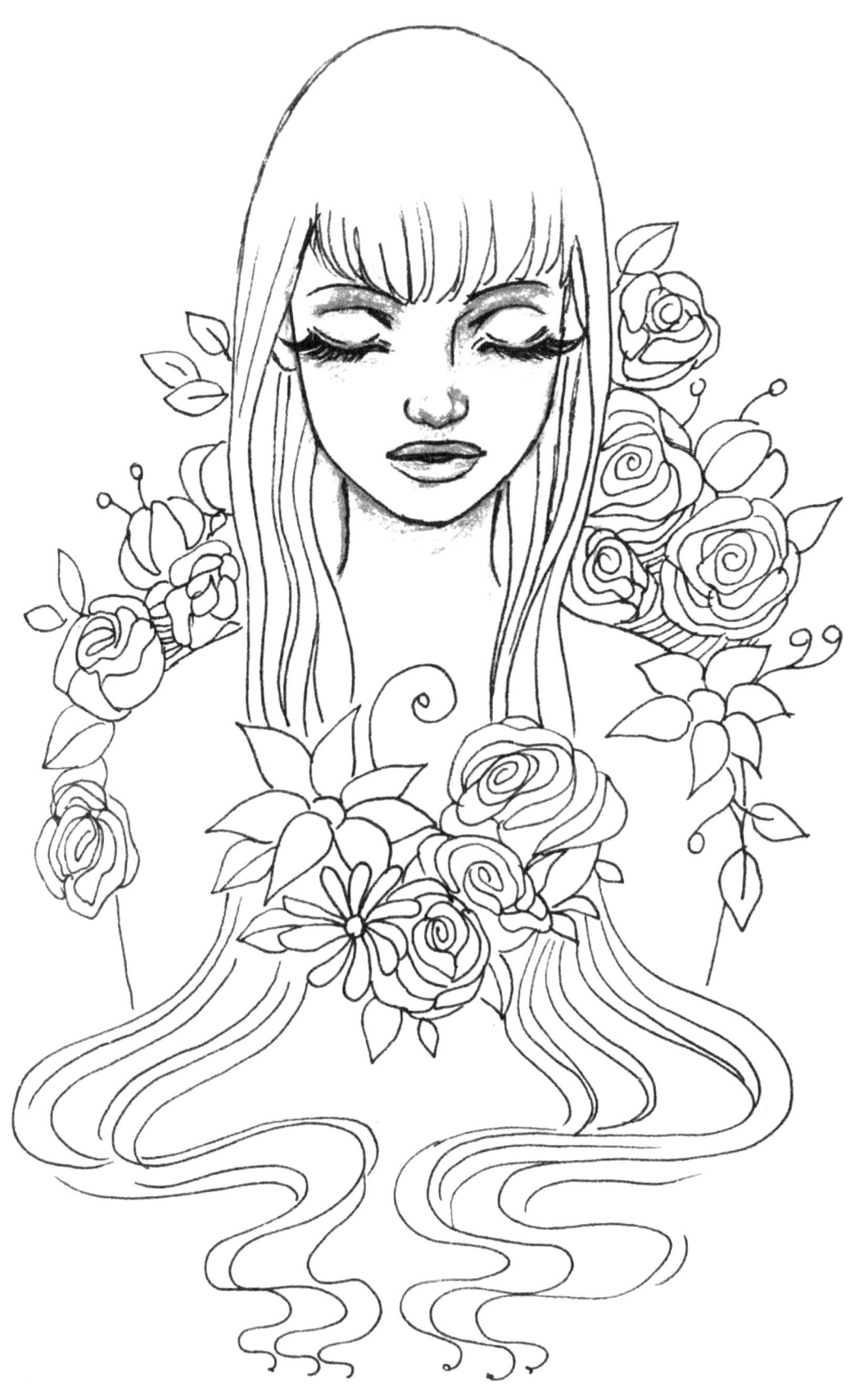

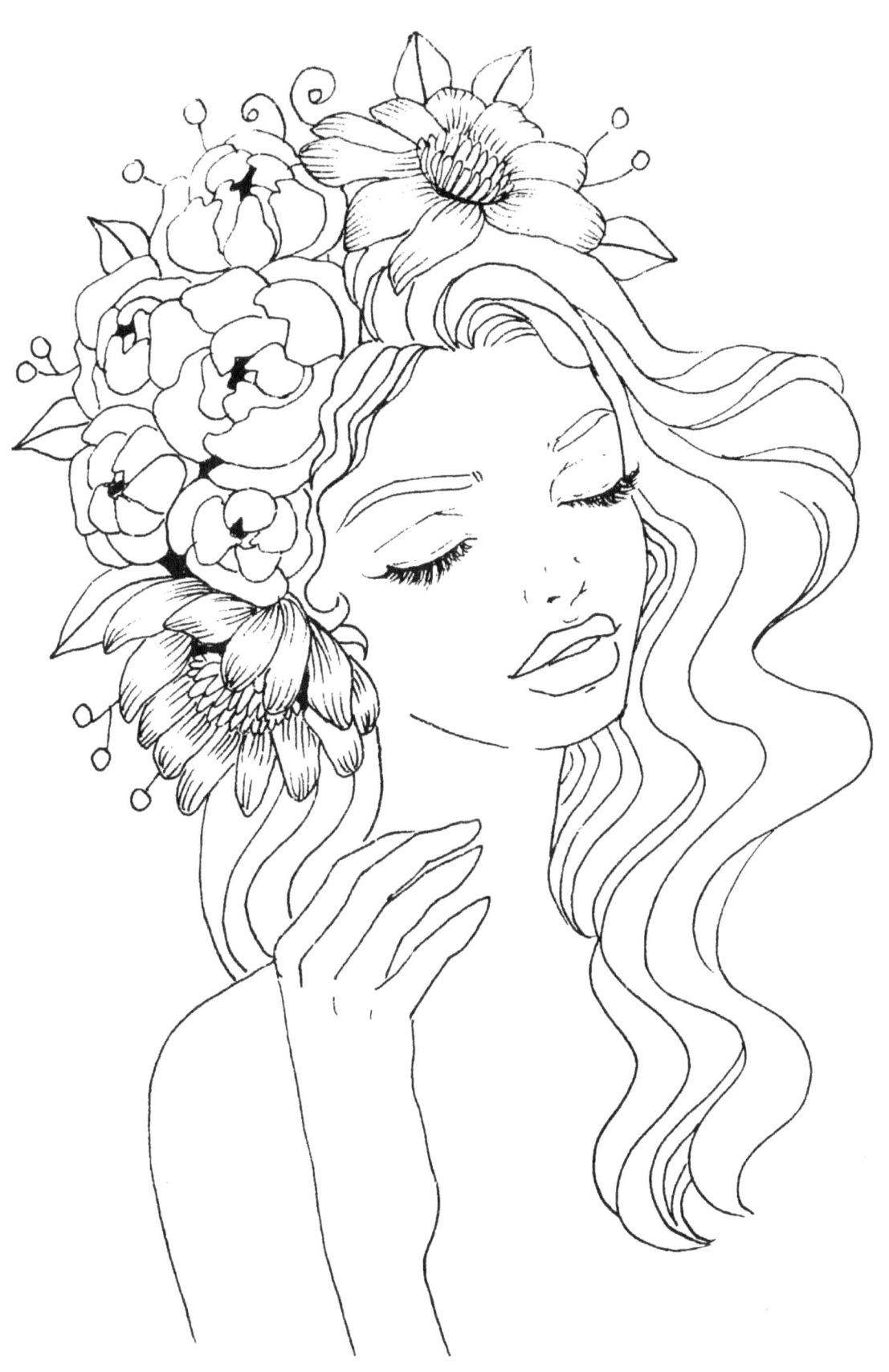

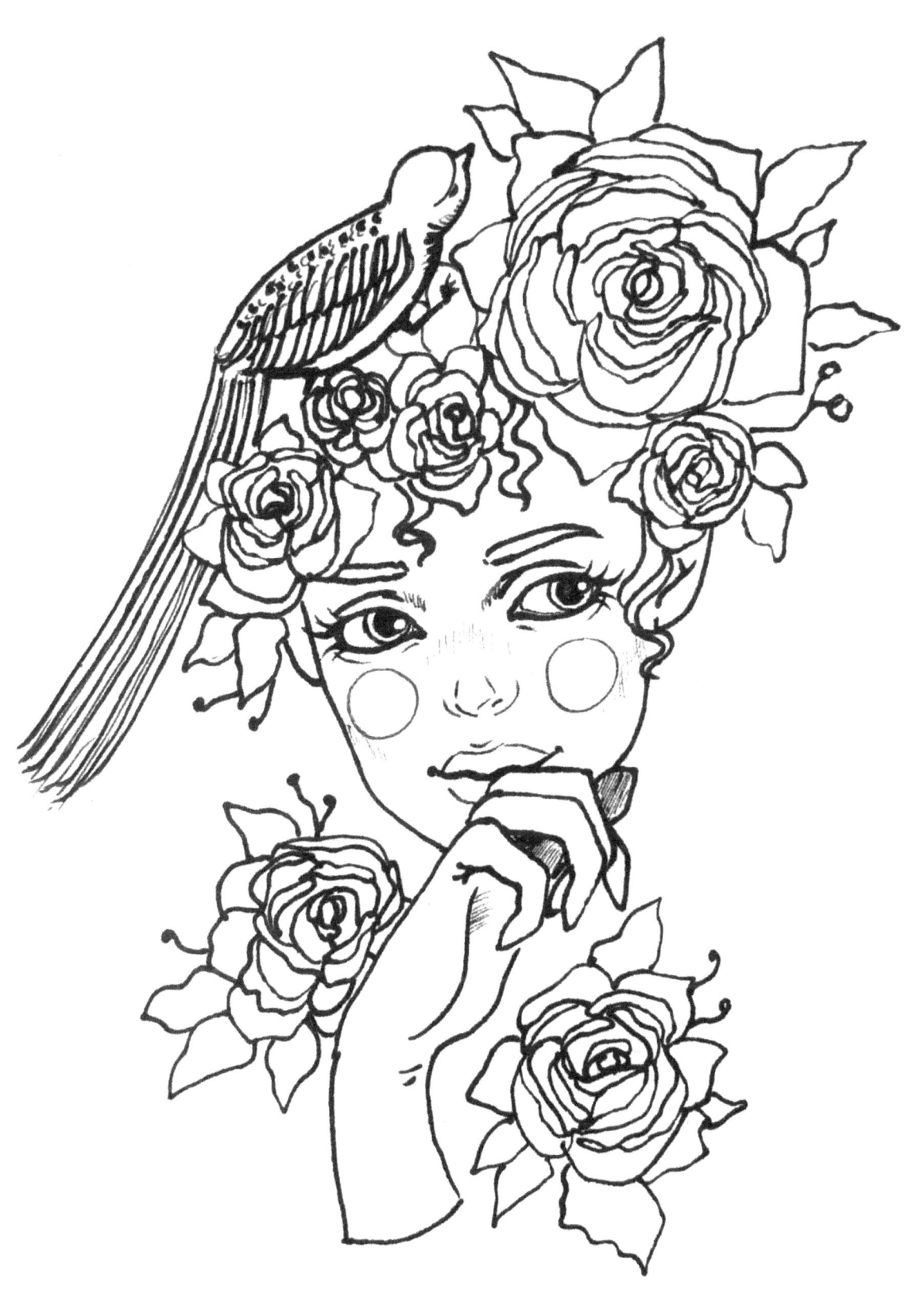

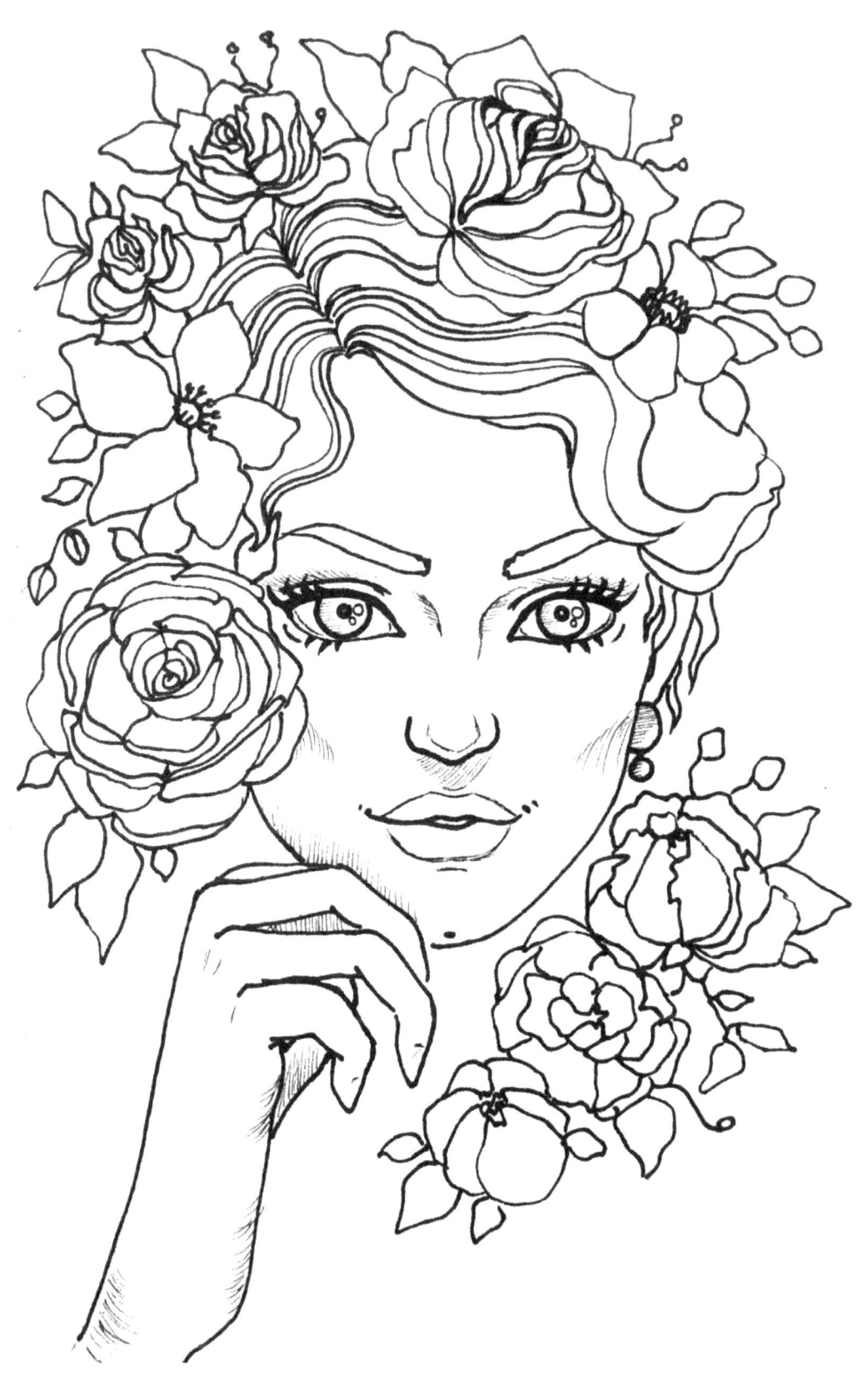

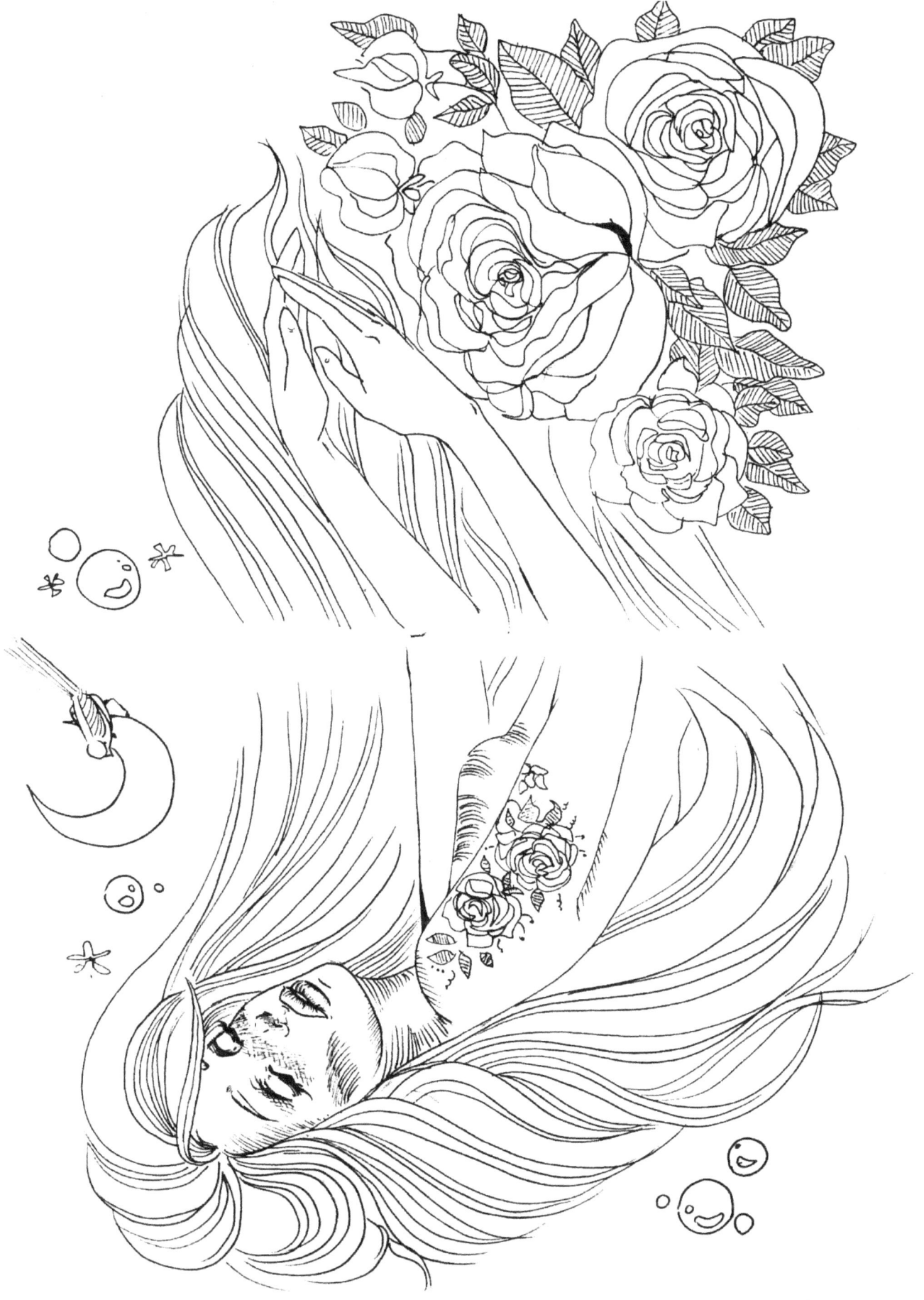

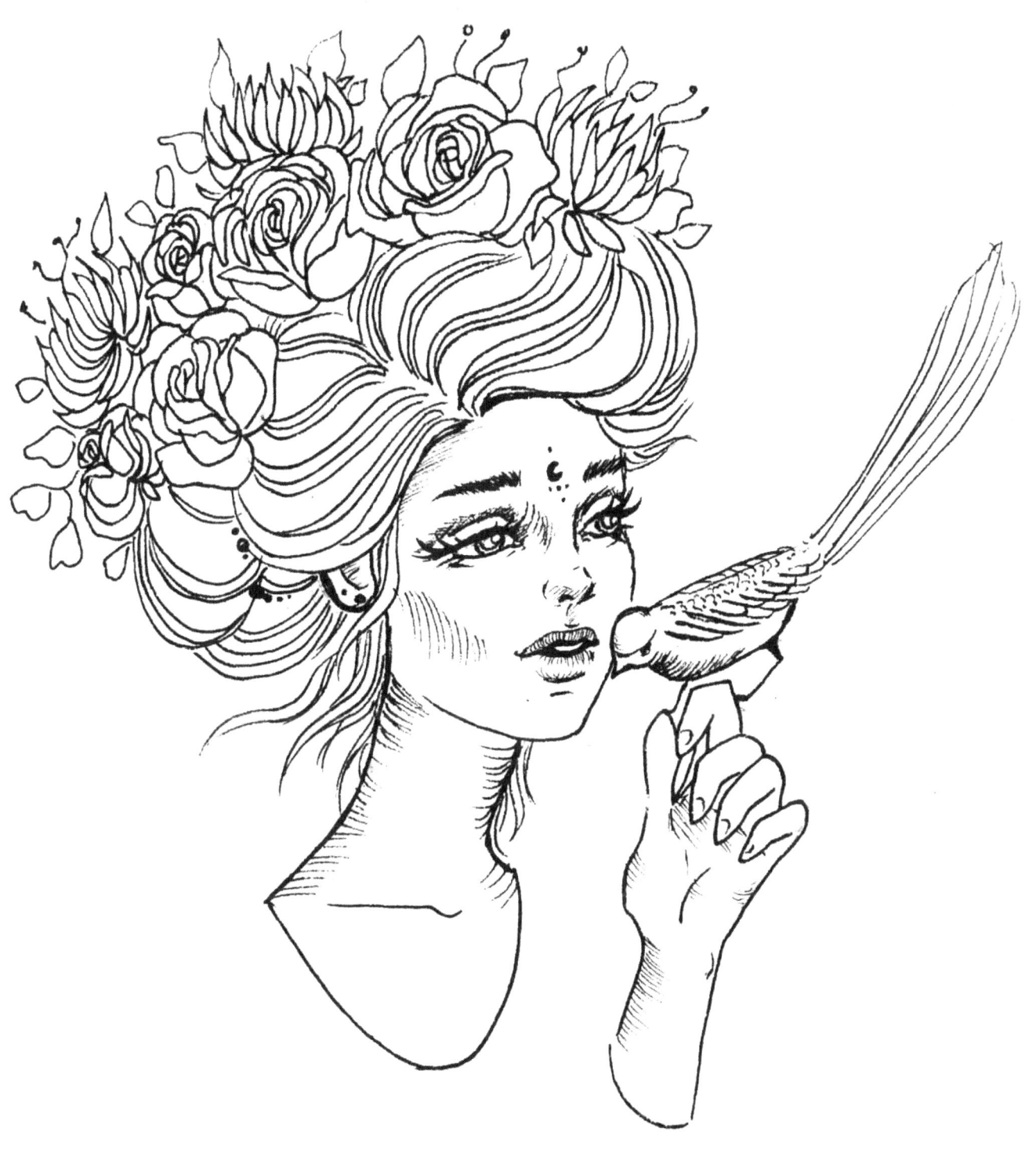

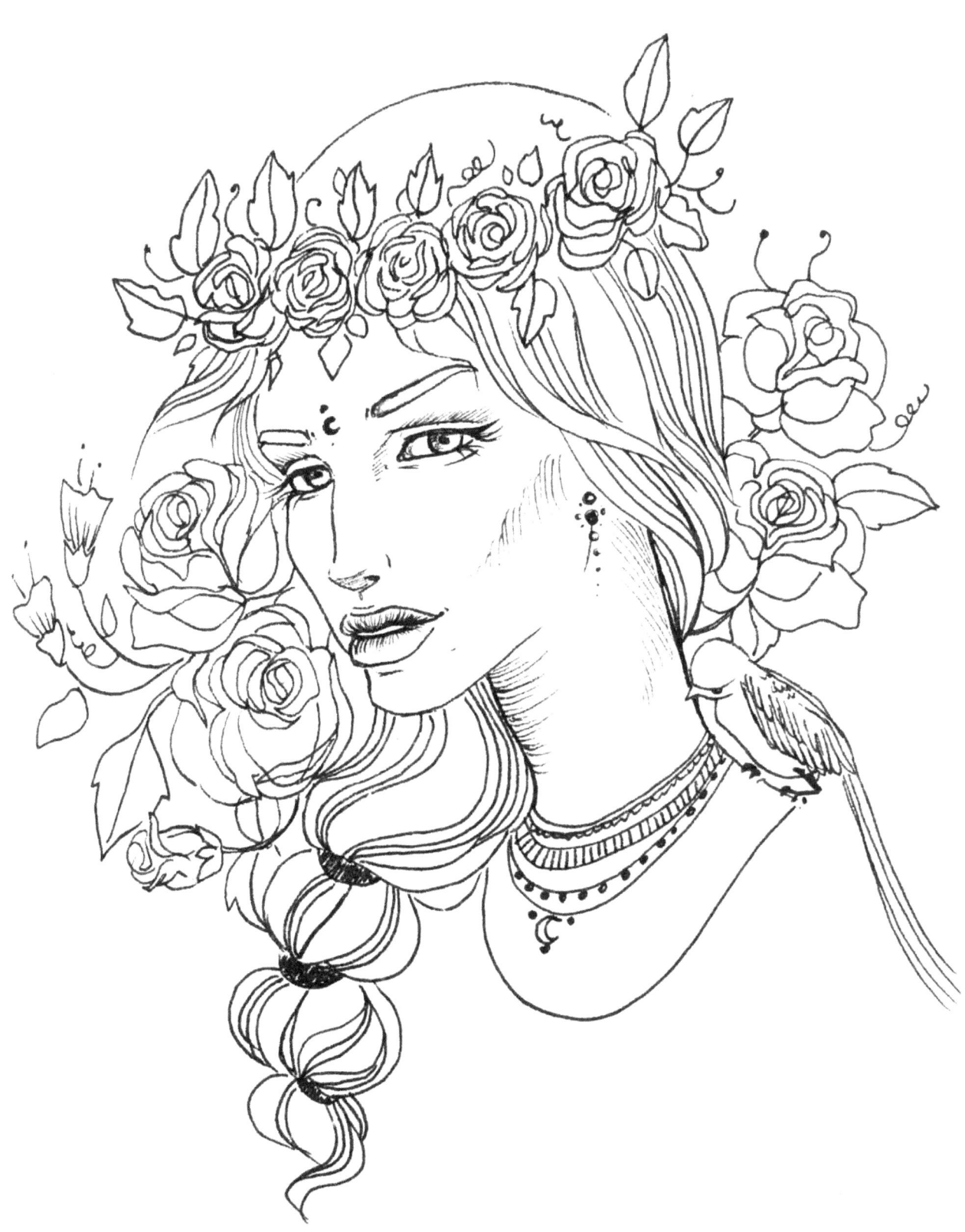

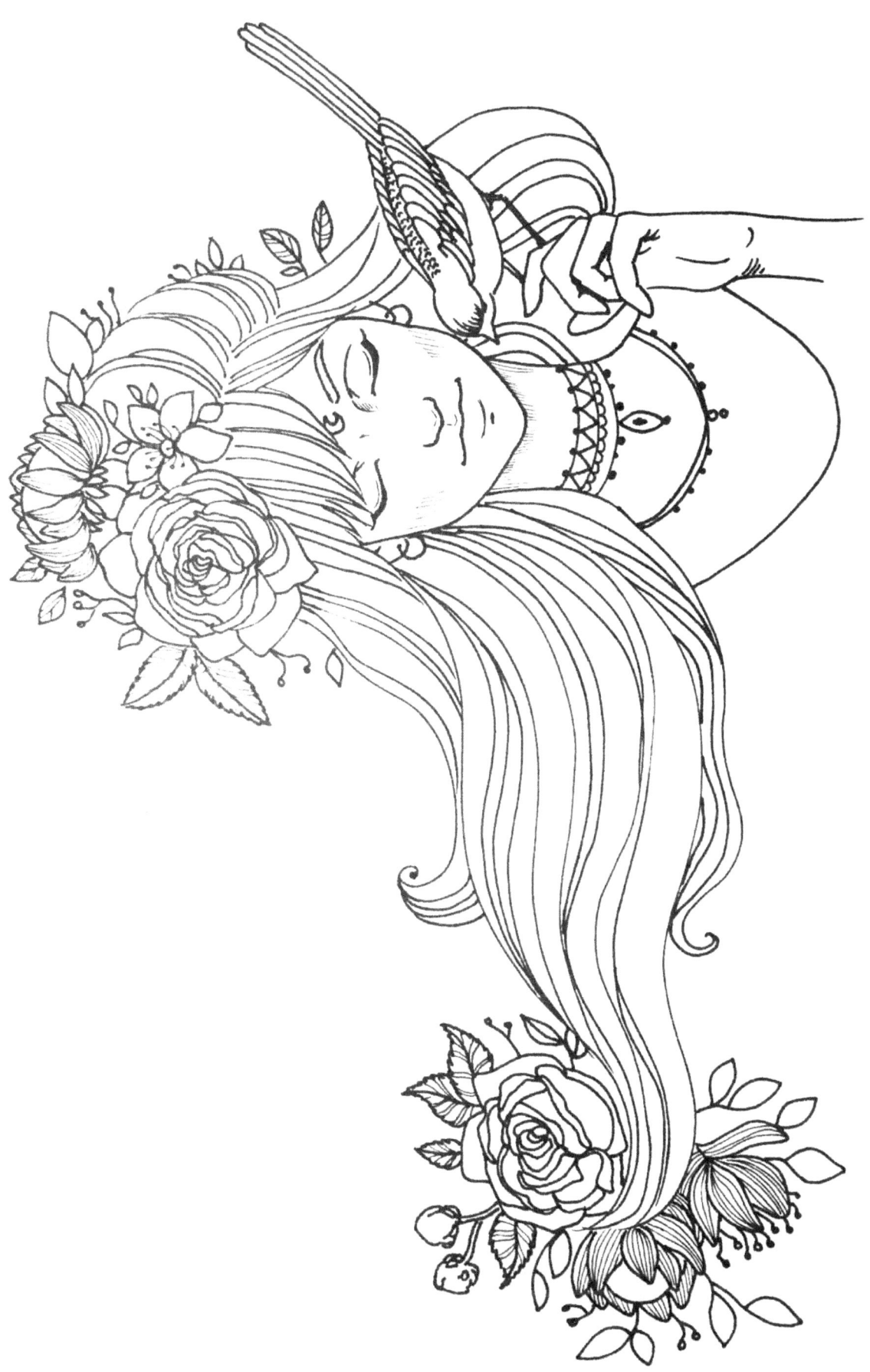

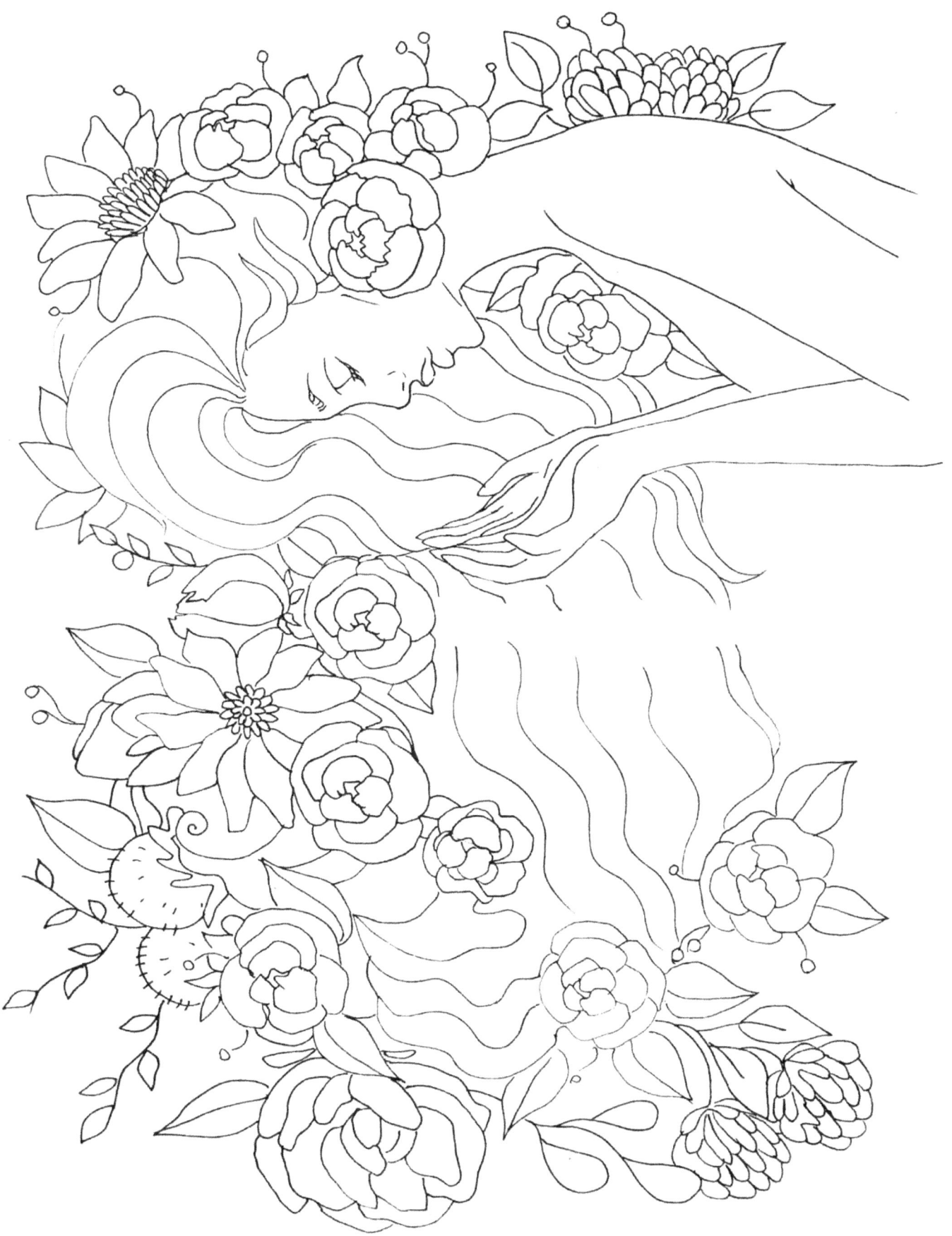

www.ingramcontent.com/pod-product-compliance
Lightning Source LLC
Chambersburg PA
CBHW081200180526
45170CB00006B/2166